# Two-Way Prayer

## Make It a Two-way Prayer

You're troubled and worried,
    you don't know what to do,
So you seek GOD in prayer
    and He listens to you,
But you seldom pause
    to let GOD speak—
You just want the answer
    that you desperately seek . . .
And after you've pleaded,
    you don't give GOD a chance
To discuss the best way
    to meet your circumstance
And you really miss
    the best part of prayer—
Which is feeling and knowing
    GOD'S PRESENCE IS THERE . . .
For so few of us linger
    to quietly share
The "SILENT COMMUNION"
    that fills the air
In which GOD is speaking
    and telling us why
Sometimes there's no answer
    to our immediate cry . . .
So pause for a while
    and just silently wait
And give GOD a chance
    to communicate,
For TWO-WAY PRAYER
    forms a JOYOUS RELATION
When we listen to GOD
    in "SHARED MEDITATION."

*Helen Steiner Rice*

# Two-Way Prayer

## Priscilla Brandt

Foreword by Joyce Landorf

**WORD BOOKS**
PUBLISHER
WACO, TEXAS

I want to express special thanks to Dr. Clifton W. King, Tarzana, California, for the many insights into Two-way Prayer gained under his tutelage.

Two-way Prayer

Copyright © 1979 by Word, Inc., Waco, Texas

ISBN 0-8499-2877-X

Library of Congress Catalog Card Number: 78–65802

*Printed in the United States of America*

A happy family is but an
earlier heaven. This book is
dedicated to my early heaven . . .

Don
   Rusty
      Sandy
         Doug

# *Foreword*

Perky Brandt's book, *Two-way Prayer,* is not a book for everyone.

It's not a fun, frothy little how-to-pray manual.

It's not a book you read to give your sagging spirits a lift or to net yourself a blessing.

It's a book for *thinking* Christians who want to avoid the stereotyped clichés on prayer and who will not settle for an ineffective, inadequate yo-yo type prayer life.

When Perky Brandt, wife, mother, and registered nurse asks:

> "If there was a way for you to go into the very presence of God where you could speak to him, and in that same moment get his direct answer— a way that would not be frightening, mysterious, or fanciful, but a way that would make you feel confident and good, you'd like to know about it, wouldn't you?"

The Christian who is willing to grow, develop, and mature in Christ shouts back a resounding "Yes!"

This book, then, is for you!!

And me,

*Joyce Landorf*

# *Contents*

*Gratefully.* . . .

It was Shakespeare who said, "Some are born great; some achieve greatness; and some have greatness thrust upon them."

God blessed me with six friends who were born great. Without their natural and loving intellect, and generosity in giving of themselves, this book would not be in your hands. I want to thank beautiful Mary Kuiper, who gently prodded me, typed my manuscript twice, and labored on a day-to-day basis to help me meet the deadline; also typists Ruth Anderson and Joyce Katsma.

Another person born great is Mrs. Phyllis Albee, head of the English Department of Loy Norrix High School in Kalamazoo, Michigan. Her brilliant mind and sense of humor were invaluable to me as she crossed out, corrected, and reworded portions of the manuscript. Since she is an author in her own right, her help gave this book readability. I also want to thank Dr. Frank Hutchinson for his priceless encouragement. Most of all, I want to thank my husband, Donald Brandt. It seems the writing of this book has brought out his true character, one of patience and wisdom. I am grateful to God for these six.

# Introduction

My discoveries in *Two-way Prayer* are the result of a lifelong search for answers in three areas: spiritual, medical, and psychological. It all started with a spiritual search. Prayer had intrigued me. I knew it was powerful. Although God always gave me what I asked for, what I did not understand was the reason I did not pray more. Why was it so boring and fatiguing to pray? I found that the longest I could pray was fifteen or twenty minutes—yet my mother prayed an hour or two every day! Through her powerful prayers six children and her husband learned to walk hand-in-hand with Christ. We used to tease mom and accuse her of catnapping. I thought it was utterly impossible to pray that long.

I was also puzzled by the prayer life of Susan Wesley. She was the mother of eighteen children, among them Charles, who was one of England's foremost hymnists and evangelists; and also John, outstanding evangelist and founder of Methodism. Allegedly, Susan Wesley sat in her living room every afternoon and threw her apron up over her head. Thus she prayed for an hour and a half. The children knew that when mother was in her rocking chair she was not to be disturbed. Her prayers conquered England . . . but how could she sit so long?

My search for answers spread beyond the spiritual to the medical. I can remember wanting to be a nurse at the early age of six. As a child I had a deep feeling of concern for the pain others experienced. I remember roller-skating with a group of neighborhood friends on a hill one hot Michigan afternoon. One of the girls fell and skinned her knee. She began to cry. Just then an ice truck drove up and parked near us. Everyone forgot the wounded friend and roller-skated toward the truck to get a chip of ice. They called to me to join them, but something inside told me this friend needed help. As badly as I wanted a chip of ice, I turned to help the girl with the bleeding knee. It was not the heroine in me that called me to her side. I simply didn't have a choice. She was hurt and I *could not* leave her alone.

As the years passed I grew more intrigued with the wonders and phenomena of the human body. Eventually I became a registered nurse. My interests were particularly drawn to the area of pain alleviation. While in nurse's training, I developed an interest in psychological nursing. Now I was involved intellectually and emotionally with three disciplines: theology, the study of God; medicine, the study of the body; and psychology, the study of the mind. For twenty-two years I have involved myself in these three disciplines. At the beginning of my research, it seemed they were thousands of miles apart. Although all three were seeking to help man, they seemed to be such bitter enemies. It was disconcerting and frustrating. One day, I hoped we would be able to treat the whole man—that medicine would see its patients as people with minds and souls as well as bodies; that psychology would be sensitive to spiritual needs and answers, as well as mental; and that Christianity would not regard the body as something bad, but rather as something to respect and love. Also, I hoped that Christianity would recognize this truth—when God heals a body or a mind he can use the physician or psychologist. Most of us in the sciences knew these shortcomings but plodded on in our meager attempts to help people.

People became my hobby. The more I learned about God, the more I loved people. I studied and interviewed them. I worked, played, and lived with them. As a pastor's wife and a registered nurse, I was with people—counseling, teaching, healing—twenty-four hours a day.

Finally, after the preliminary preparation of my own soul, the breakthrough came. My soul's reconstruction took place one night as I stood on the edge of the Pacific Ocean. We were vacationing at our cottage in Baja, Mexico. The children and Don were playing Monopoly in the "casa" (that's our cottage), and I was enjoying the solitude of the sandy shore. It was midnight and the new moon was "slivered." The ocean was calm and dark except for the waves that broke near shore. As the waves broke, their iridescent caps traveled the entire length of the cove. Stars thickened the sky and the warm southerly breezes gently moved the air. My heart was full of the beauty of God and his universe. I began humming a little chorus. The words echoed in my mind:

> Fill My house unto the fullest;
> Eat My bread and drink My wine.
> The love I bear is held from no one;
> All I have and all I do,
> I give to you.
>
> Take My time unto the fullest;
> Find in Me the trust you seek.
> Take My hand to you outreaching;
> All I have and all I am,
> I give to you.
>
> Christ our Lord with love enormous
> From the cross this lesson taught:
> Love all men as I have loved you;
> All I have, and all I am
> I give to you.
>
> Join in me as one in Christ's love;
> May our hearts all beat as one.
> May we give ourselves completely;
> All I have, and all I am,
> I give to you.
>
> *Author Unknown*

I stopped singing and thought, *All I have, and all I am—I give to you.* That's enormous! Does Christ mean that? Does he give us his total self "to be" and "to do"? I remembered the scripture that says, "Greater works than these shall he do" (John 14:12). Didn't he say in the Beatitudes that we would inherit the earth, that we would be fulfilled, that we would have power within? Then why was I living in such a rut with my Christianity? I remember crying to God, "You're big, and powerful, and beautiful. Teach me more about Yourself. If You were to 'fill me' as the chorus says, and 'give me' all You are and have, I would explode! I'm so small compared to You."

But what made me small? My own self-made boundaries? My fears, prejudices, and preconceived ideas—especially in judging people? I cried and prayed, "Oh, God, break down my skeptical mental barriers. Help me believe everything, everybody, every miracle. Help me to be open and innocent toward You. In Jesus' name. Amen."

That prayer was more significant than I knew at the time. Without believing, I never would have "seen God." God answered my desire to know more of him in a most unexpected way.

When our vacation was over, I returned to the doctors' office where I was working. There in a medical journal I found an article headlined, "Biofeedback Cures Tension Migraine Headaches."

*Anything that cures tension headaches I want to know more about. . . . what's biofeedback?* I wondered. I talked with Dr. Gary Voorman, M.D., psychiatrist, who is head of the Psychiatric Department at San Antonio Hospital in California. Dr. Voorman was just starting to use biofeedback in one of his three clinics. He introduced me to his technician who was trained to administer biofeedback exercises.

Dr. Voorman and his staff were gracious and easy to work with. Since the doctors I worked for had their offices next to his, it was convenient for me. I worked for Dr. Fred Gattas and Dr. R. N. Williams (who is the head of the Coronary Care Unit at San Antonio Hospital). I did case studies on patients referred to Dr. Voorman for biofeedback training. It was exciting to see how helpful biofeedback was in many illnesses—mental and physical.

Then I was invited to take the course in biofeedback offered to medical schools across our country. I was excited because it was taught by Dr. Barbara Brown, world's foremost authority on biofeedback, at the University of California. The class was filled with 250 psychiatrists and physicians—and a few outsiders like me!

Paralleling my study in biofeedback, about the same time I began reading medical bulletins dealing with the research being done in meditation. The study was being conducted by the Harvard Medical School. A statement from this prestigious school said, "Meditation is the greatest cure for anxiety." What effect would it have on the millions of dollars spent on tranquilizers, I wondered. I felt a glimmer of hope as I thought of the possible reduction in the escalating use of Valium and other drugs employed to deal with peoples' emotions. Claims also were made that meditation was helping to lower blood pressure, and improve physical and mental health. I looked for a class of formal study in meditation. Dr. Clifton King, one of the nation's greatest authorities in meditation, invited my husband and me to be guests in his class.

Something dynamic was beginning. Biofeedback was dealing mostly with the objective and cognitive effects of relaxation upon the physical body; Dr. King, a Christ-centered lecturer at the University of Southern California, was teaching the spiritual and psychological effects of relaxation. Since I'm skeptical by nature, God knew I had to experience first-hand the benefits the researchers were claiming.

As I did the biofeedback and meditative exercises, I turned my thoughts toward God. I found if I quieted my mind before entering my inner prayer closet, beautiful things happened. I began to experience a feeling of closeness to God—a feeling that I could stretch forth my hand and God would take hold of it. I didn't see anyone with my eyes, but I felt a loving presence so real and close it brought inner peace and joy to my troubled soul. I felt the Presence inside of me and outside of me, all around me, above and beyond me. I have since recognized this kind of perception as the "hereness" of God. I believe, now, the "hereness" of God is always present but that I'm not always tuned into it. Now I was learning how to develop a sensitivity to his presence. I was also learning the mechanisms that prevented the feelings of closeness. The intriguing part for me came when I

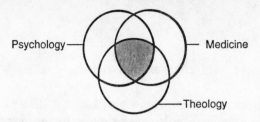

Psychology — Medicine

Theology

was in prayer and I could ask God a question, then immediately the thought-answer would slip smoothly into my mind. The answers were wise and loving.

Although this experience was exciting, I was not ready to talk about it to anyone. I called it *Two-way Prayer,* because I talked to God and he talked back. I started to study the acts of prayer by saints of old and saints of today. I read Frank Laubach, Romano Guardine, Francois Biot, I also read *The Spiritual Exercises of St. Ignatius* and *The Rule of Taize.* They seemed quite mystical and vague for my scientific mind. Nevertheless, I was thrilled to learn that one of the growing edges of medicine, and one of the growing edges of psychology, were coming together with theology. Now the threads of body, mind, and spirit were intermingling in scientific agreement. The three disciplines found a common core. Dr. King, who lectures internationally to top government officials and key corporation heads on stress release, was tying the threads for me. As he lectured on the levels of the mind, he defined my inner experiences. Dr. King taught me the conditions of the mind that kept *Two-way Prayer* working. It was all based on scripture. He taught me to detect negative emotions and to deal with them. Since Dr. King has studied psychology for twenty years and has taught meditation for thirty years, his experience and wisdom have been invaluable to me in my search for truth.

Now I travel the country, teaching the concepts of *Two-way Prayer.* These teachings are universally accepted. It seems people have an innate feeling that *Two-way Prayer* is valid. Many, who had unknowingly experienced this kind of prayer earlier in their lives as I had, are thrilled to have it defined and given biblical structure. As a nurse, I am excited that prayer also has medical and psychological benefits. (That sounds just like something God would do!) Our generation is ready to know God intimately in an experiential, scriptural way. We are ready for *Two-way Prayer.*

# 1

# The Secret of
# Two-way Prayer

Thousands of years ago the secret of Two-way Prayer was tucked away in Psalm 46:10. It says, "Be still, and know that I am God." Most people thought "be still" meant motion stillness, but we know it to be more than this. A person may be motionless, but his muscles can still be tense. Or one may have motion stillness, muscular relaxation, mental calmness, and still have spiritual turbulence. One may not yet know God. The command, "Be still, and know that I am God," calls for physical, mental, and spiritual harmony. When the body is still and the mind totally quiet, we can become sensitive to the wise and creative thoughts God gives to help us through life. From technology we know that this kind of relaxation heals the destructive results of its counterpart, tension. One can be healed physically, psychologically, and spiritually. These are the benefits of Two-way Prayer.

## The Highest Form of Prayer

Two-way Prayer is not simply a new name to add to our list of names for prayer. It is a different form of prayer to add to our lives.

Spiritual development requires that we grow in our prayer lives. We have experienced three forms of prayer: *praise, petition,* and *intercession.* Sometimes we just want to meditate on the greatness and marvel at the power of God. Our hearts lift in *praise* when we pray. Again, in times of crisis when we don't know what to do, we just breathe a prayer of *petition*—a one-way prayer asking God to help us. The third form—*intercession*—

comes when we go to God with our list of friends, family members or the enemy who are hurting. In all of these forms we are pleading and talking *to* God.

The fourth and highest form that I have found is Two-way Prayer—sitting comfortably in quiet meditation, taking time to come into the presence of God, and actually having God communicate with me. It is a fascinating, rewarding, and beautiful experience. We may not all share our intellectual capacity with the world, or our leadership ability, or our true beauty, but we can all learn to walk hand-in-hand with God without arrogance or fear.

Teaching students this intimate relationship with God was the aim of our Two-way Prayer Seminars. One evening I walked into a church sanctuary to speak to about a hundred students waiting eagerly to learn the technique. I said, "If there was a way to have God speak to you that wouldn't frighten or scare you—would you want to know it?" A mass nodding of heads told me I must share this treasured experience with others.

After class a dentist walked up to me and said, "Perky, I know what you are saying is true, but I haven't had time to develop skill in prayer as you have. I have a patient I'm terribly concerned about. Could you go into Two-way Prayer and ask God if there's anything more I can do for her? She has an abscessed tooth and it's so bad her cheek and eye are swollen and red. I've done a root-canal and she's on antibiotics. She seems to get worse by the hour."

I told him I wasn't sure if God would give me answers for other people, but I would try.

That evening when I went into Two-way Prayer, I asked God about the patient. God told me he wanted Frank, the dentist, to learn to speak face-to-face with him, but that if Frank would have the patient apply moist heat it would get better.

"Moist heat, Lord! On an abscess? Isn't that just the *wrong* thing to do to a closed abscess?"

The Lord answered, "Heat, Perky."

The next morning I couldn't bring myself to call my dentist friend. I was sure he would lose all confidence in Two-way Prayer at such a ridiculous answer. Because of my doubts, I went into Two-way Prayer again, "Lord, is there anything else Frank can do for that abscess?"

"Heat!"

"Heat? That might spread the infection to the brain, Lord."

"Heat! *Heat!* HEAT!" came the answer back in large red thoughts!

I felt that if Two-way Prayer were valid, I had to act on the inspiration God gave, no matter how senseless it might seem to me.

Calling Dr. Hutchinson, I told him that God had said "moist heat."

There was a long, uncomfortable silence. My mind was saying, "Oh, Perky! You're only a registered nurse—what do you know about dental problems!?"

Then Dr. Hutchinson cleared his throat and said, "Well, ordinarily heat is contraindicated in an abscessed tooth, but if God said 'heat,' we'll apply heat."

The patient was better in forty-eight hours! Later Dr. Hutchinson and I were discussing the basic principles of heat.

"In the internist's office where you work, Perky, do you ever use heat on a similar type of infection?" Frank asked.

"Not really," I replied, "although in the case of infected sinuses, we tell our patients to place moist heat over the sinus areas across the cheeks and forehead. This helps congestion because there is a natural opening for the drainage."

"Oh," he said, "I forgot to tell you. I had made a surgical opening into that abscess but it wouldn't drain! With that surgical opening moist heat would be the treatment of choice!"

*Companion in Prayer*

Isn't it great that when we have a Close Friend, we can ask a question and then sit back and listen to our Friend's answer—an answer we can trust to be wise and true? This is what I have found in Two-way Prayer. I learned how much he wants to help all of us find our way if only we put his natural laws to work. Throughout the Bible he has told mankind, century after century, the laws of successful prayer. Few have found it, but everyone can have it if he really wants it.

However, some of our early feelings about God have made him approachable only in a formal ritual and with fear. One day after a seminar, a middle-aged woman stated she liked the idea of Two-way Prayer but she could not relax. "The idea of almighty God's speaking to me makes me afraid," she admitted. When she learned that her fear itself could be expressed to her Friend who had all power, she entered the presence of God with the trust of a two-year-old youngster snuggling into her father's arms in the dark.

There is a way we can go into the very presence of God to speak to him, and in that very moment get his direct answer. Not at all mysterious, fanciful or frightening, this way makes us feel confident and good.

### Inter-com to God

Two-way Prayer is simply talking to God and then listening. It's the listening part that's exciting but needs to be respected. One can train oneself to be sensitive to God's thoughts by entering into the inner stillness of the soul. The *inner-calm*, free from the harrassment of negative thoughts, becomes the *inter-com* to God. There we find creative answers to our problems, a source of joy, strength, and peace—there we find God! There are steps to follow that will bring us into God's presence where we can talk with him and he with us. The preparation for successful Two-way Prayer begins with the way we approach God.

### The Way We Approach God

Moses approached God and had beautiful fellowship with him. We are told that Enoch and Noah both "walked with God." The psalmist also felt God's presence which brought strength and comfort. "The Lord is nigh unto all them that call upon him" (Ps. 145:18). For effective Two-way Prayer we need to believe that God is our friend. Jesus needed to reassure his followers that he wanted to be considered their friend, too. "Henceforth I call you not servants; for the servant knoweth not what his Lord doeth: but I have called you friends for all things that I have heard of my Father I have made known unto you" (John 15:15).

It's awesome to realize that the God who created more than one hundred thousand galaxies is our Friend; furthermore, he wants to talk with us.

He wants to share with us his wisdom to help us better understand life.

Isaiah says, "You have advisors by the ton—your astrologers and stargazers, who try to tell you what the future holds. But they are as useless as dried grass burning in the fire" (Isa. 47:13 LB). God wants to be our Guide. Why do we look to secondary sources?

## Lines Too Busy

He wants to tell us day by day the things that will make us become the kind of persons we want to be. But most of the time he can't be heard. He just can't get through. When we go to God in prayer, we often shut him out—not because we want to, but because we talk too much. Do our prayers filibuster heaven? We need to learn to be silent. We ask a question and then another and another and another ". . . in Jesus' name. Amen." We're so busy asking questions that by the time God answers the first question, we're busily asking the second . . . and the third!

Have you ever talked with people who act like that? They ask you how you are and before you can answer, they ask you how your trip was. You start to tell them about your trip and they ask how your mother is! What do you do? You stop trying to answer them and just listen to their questions. Those people need to learn to ask a question and wait for the answer.

We, too, need to learn to ask God a question and wait for an answer. We can learn to listen for God's answers as my friend in Pomona, California, did.

## God's Partner in Business

Pete owned his own welding business. The roller coaster of his business determined his attitude at home. In good times he was buoyant; in bad, he was despondent. At times he blamed himself, felt worthless and far from God. His despair shadowed . his home, his social, and his spiritual life. *His business ran him.*

Pete had symptoms similar to heart disease. A checkup with his doctor proved there was nothing organically wrong. The doctor warned him he had to learn to relax. Physically, mentally, and spiritually he was a taut rubber band. Tenseness, a way of life for Pete, was becoming a way to death.

Out of curiosity, he came to a Two-way Prayer seminar in Pomona, Caifornia. Tentatively, he followed the instructions. First he learned to relax his body, then his mind, and, finally, his soul (through the technique of Two-way Prayer).

When he met Jesus in prayer, it was an instant love relationship. The historical Jesus who lived two thousand years ago became so vivid to Pete that he felt he could touch him. Pete became emotionally involved in a beautiful oneness with Christ. No longer would prayer be only the occasional peak experience common to many Christians. Having learned the techniques of Two-way Prayer, Pete could have a personal encounter with Jesus whenever he prayed. When Jesus becomes real to a person, the individual radiates. Pete did. His business friends, acquaintances, and even his family noticed a deep joy that sustained him even through business setbacks. During one of those setbacks, Pete went to the Lord and asked why his business was slow. Jesus said, "Don't worry about it. By the end of the week you'll have so much business you'll have to hire a new man to help you."

A short time later, an experienced welder came to him for work. Pete had the faith to say, "I think I'll need a new man in a few days." He hired him. By the end of the week, Pete had more work than he could have handled without this additional help. Starting each exciting day with prayer, he received orders and advice from God. He told me, "It's like God is a real partner in my business now. I ask him about expanding;

where to move my business; or what building to rent. One day I read an ad for a building that is larger than the one I have. I asked God if I should move into that building. God told me not to because it wouldn't be suitable. When I went to see the building, it was old and in poor repair—not at all adequate. I could have saved time by listening to God's whisper. It takes a while to trust God and save time!"

Pete told me he spends about ten minutes in Two-way Prayer as soon as he gets to the office. Then he sets to work and works hard. That's the secret! Prayer and work, work and prayer, and his business is thriving. A year after the beginning of their partnership, Pete had moved into a beautiful new building. His and God's welding business continues to grow.

## God's Partner in Creativity

A creative answer to a business problem came to Pete one day in prayer. Growing bored with the tedious welding of dairy equipment and farm implements, he told the Lord he was tired of it. Immediately an innovative plan came to his mind.

"Pete, you've always liked antique cars. Even as a young boy you played with antique models. Why don't you weld and build replicas of antique cars as a side business?"

Pete knew, in every level of his being, that this would work! He knew he could do it. There was a market for it. As fast as he could create a replica, he could sell it! He was excited about his new sideline. "Furthermore," he said, "it doesn't seem right to get paid for something that's fun to do!"

Isn't God just like that? He wants us to enjoy our work. He cares about the businessman, and he delights in seeing his children productive and successful. This is all part of God's personality. God is productive and undefeatable. God is abundant, not miserly. He is strength, not weakness. He is success, not failure.

## God's Partner in Success

God cares about the success of the wife and mother, too. One day I received a telephone call from a mother who had learned the technique of Two-way Prayer during the National Women's Convention for Possibility Thinkers at Garden Grove Church in California. This was her story:

"My son is not a good student and he dearly loves sports. I wanted him to spend more time on his school work so he could stay in sports activities. Sports were the only effective stimulus we had found to motivate him to study harder. If he kept his grades high, he could qualify for the team. It was working beautifully!

"Then, against my wishes, my husband gave my son permission to have a paper route. I deeply resented my husband's decision to encourage the paper route. It meant my son would have to drop out of the sports program!

"Last night, as my son was getting the papers ready to deliver on his new route, it began to rain. He had to put plastic bags around each paper. Then he couldn't find his route book. It was late in the afternoon and it was growing dark. I was busy getting supper ready when he came to me and said, 'Mom, since dad is out of town and I'm late delivering my papers, and it's raining outside, will you drive me around my route?'

"I thought, *Who will watch my supper to keep it from burning? If I stop cooking it, supper will be two hours late! I'm tired and I don't want to go out in the cold, wet rain, anyway!* But . . . I didn't have a choice! I was seething with anger! I slammed through the house looking for his route book. His sister and younger brother were frantically turning over the cushions of the furniture. The dog coop? The trash can? Under the bed? I felt desperate and helpless! We looked everywhere for that book!

"Finally, at the point of exhaustion, I decided to go into Two-way Prayer. I told the children I wanted to be left absolutely alone for twenty minutes. I wanted to pray. I remembered you had taught us how resentments and anger could block our communication with God . . . and I had a barrel of them! So after letting go of all my tensions, my body began to relax. Then my mind started to quiet down. I knew I had to deal with the resentments I had for my husband and the paper route. I also had to get rid of my anger at being interrupted during the rush hour of supper. I asked God to forgive me. With the bitterness removed, the channels were clear.

"Then I asked God if he would tell me where the route book was. He said in quiet, loving thoughts, *It's in the lower cupboard next to the refrigerator. It was put in the junk drawer and fell out the back and into the cupboard below.* Since I had now regained my composure I went quietly downstairs, looked in the cupboard next to the refrigerator, and, Perky, you won't believe this, but there it was. The route book was there! In the cupboard, just as Jesus said! Isn't he terrific?"

The thrill of finding the route book was great, but greater still was the knowledge that God does care about what concerns us.

### God's Partner in Reassurance

This kind of dialogue with Christ is not a new prayer concept. It's quite old, in fact. All the secrets of effective prayer are in the Bible. The majority of us have glibly read over them, failing to handle these principles with respect, or completely misunderstanding them. The concept is so old, in fact, that we read about Two-way Prayer in ancient scripture.

Beautiful, sensitive Rebecca, Isaac's beloved wife, became pregnant after years of waiting (Gen. 25:23). After a few months she noticed an excessive amount of movement and turmoil within her. She must have felt as if she were carrying a monster with four arms and four legs! In despair she cried to the Lord, "I can't endure this!"

The Lord answered and reassured her it was no monster. She was carrying twins. "And the elder shall serve the younger" (Gen. 25:23). He gave her understanding and peace. That's Two-way Prayer—asking a question and receiving insight.

A Reformed Church minister came to me after class one night and said, "Perky, this Two-way Prayer is the best thing that has happened to my spiritual life since I found Christ. I received such an enlightening answer this week it settled me right down so that I could study for my sermons!" I urged him to share his prayer experience.

"Two weeks ago," he said, "I received a 'call' to pastor another congregation. I just didn't know what God's will was concerning this decision. I've been agonizing in prayer ever since. It consumes my every waking moment. I love my present congregation and hate to think of leaving them. Yet the need in the other church is equally great. I felt torn between the two. When I went to prayer, I asked God what he wanted me to do about 'the call'? He said to me, 'I'm not ready to tell you yet!' Do you know what that did for me? I totally relaxed. If he wasn't ready to tell me yet, why should I force the answer? I was able to go about my work with a new freedom." What a relief he felt when God shared his simplest plan with him.

There was a prophet several thousand years ago who was in a state of great anxiety, too. His name was Elijah. He used Two-way Prayer to find relief. In deep trouble, he was weary of fighting his professional peers. He seemed to be the only prophet who worshiped the Lord God of Israel. As far as he knew, at least, he was the only one who did. It's hard to stand alone against the intelligentsia of one's profession! The others worshiped the idol Baal. The prophets who were Baal worshipers organized politically to have Elijah killed. Elijah fled to the mountains for amnesty and to get his battle instructions from God. Then something terrifying happened.

"And a mighty windstorm hit the mountain; it was such a terrible blast that the rocks were torn loose . . . After the wind, there was an earthquake . . . and a blazing fire. And after the fire, there was a gentle whisper"—the whisper of God (1 Kings 19:11–13 LB).

## God's Quietness

It was not in the wind, earthquake, or fire that God spoke. In the quiet whisper of God important plans were given to Elijah which brought a nation and a king to repentance. Elijah found the power in quietness that the scripture talks about. "In quietness and confidence shall be your strength" (Isa. 30:15).

There is tremendous creative power in quietness—creative physical power, as well as creative spiritual power. Elijah found both in the stillness. He went down from the mountain and had the physical power to accomplish God's work.

In Two-way Prayer we train ourselves to retreat from the storms of life into the inner recesses of our souls where God can speak in the stillness.

The tornado has a quiet center which furnishes it with power. Our inner calm furnishes us with energetic power to be productive in any way we want to be productive! We obtain inner confidence to overcome personality weaknesses, or feelings of inferiority. Fears are turned to courage. Stress and tension are alleviated, reducing anxiety.

The psalmist also gained confidence and courage during moments of stillness. In Psalm 46:10 we read, "Be still, and know that I am God." This is enormously significant! His most treasured moments with the Lord were in the middle of the night when his body was still and the world around him was quiet. He says, "I will bless the Lord who counsels me; he gives me wisdom in the night. He tells me what to do" (Ps. 16:7 LB).

*Four Steps in Two-way Prayer*

The first step in Two-way Prayer is to *stop and let go.* David had to stop and let go of his muscular tension and activity. He had to let go of all his fretting, fearful thoughts. His taut body and disquieted mind needed God's healing. Many times David talks about praying in the middle of the night: "I lie awake at night thinking of you—of how much you have helped me" (Ps. 63:6 LB).

At other times, quieting the stressful activities of the mind was difficult for the psalmist. Once he was fleeing for his life with enemies on every side. Through no fault of his own he was filled with fear and anxiety. Nevertheless, it spoiled his intimacy with God. It caused his failure in Two-way Prayer.

In Psalm 77 he struggles:

> I cry to the Lord;
> I call and call
> to him. Oh,
> that he would
> listen. I am in
> deep trouble and I
> need his help so
> badly. All night
> long I pray . . . I am
> too distressed even
> to pray! (vv. 1–4, LB).

Have you ever been "too distressed" to pray? I have! It was extremely disturbing. I knew I needed God's help, but to receive his help I must pray . . . but I couldn't pray. I was too upset to pray! If there is a time we become too distressed to pray, we can remember that the psalmist did an interesting thing when he couldn't talk to God. He simply stopped trying! Reminiscing on the past, he did some honest soul-searching. He took inventory of the things he had done wrong in his life (see Ps. 77:5–10).

The second important step in effective Two-way Prayer is to *look at negative emotions.* Looking is the distilling process. We look within ourselves, letting God search our minds: "Search me, O God, and know my heart . . . my thoughts" (Ps. 139:23). This takes quiet contemplation. Do we have any resentments? Any fears? Any jealousies, feelings of inferiority or anger? We need to deal with each of these one by one. Is there guilt? Guilt because of wrongdoing? Or is there imagined guilt—guilt that comes as a result of something someone has told us we did wrong and we believed him? Imagined guilt needs to be examined in the loving mental presence of Christ. The human body was not designed to bear negative emotions. Confessing our guilt to Christ brings healing. "If we confess our sins he is faithful and just to forgive us our sins, and to cleanse us from all unrighteousness" (1 John 1:9).

David found God to be sensitive and loving, and very understanding (Ps. 107:1). In another psalm he asks: "But how can I ever know what sins are lurking in my heart? Cleanse me from these hidden faults. And keep me from deliberate wrongs; help me stop doing them. Only then can I be free of guilt" (Ps. 19:12, 13 LB). This catharsis cleanses the mind and psyche, or soul.

Then the third step begins the *love* process. Feeling and admitting God's love for us begins our healing. Spending time thinking of how much God loves us; what that love has meant in our lives; how it has affected our personalities; how it has affected our families, our communities, and our world is soothing and comforting to troubled, bruised psyches.

The psalmist's thoughts went back to the "good old days of the past, long since ended. Then my nights were filled with joyous songs" (Ps. 77:6 LB).

Next he contemplates all the great things God had done in his life; how God redeemed him (Ps. 81:1, 4), and the marvels of former generations. His meditation turns to praise, until in Psalm 81 he bursts out with triumph over his inner dilemma with, "The Lord makes us strong! Sing praises! Sing to Israel's God! . . . for God has given us these times of joy" (Ps. 81:1, 4, LB). This is the psalmist's affirmation and God's miraculous tranquilizer! The dark, dolorous clouds of anxiety fade into the clear blue sky of intimacy with God once more.

Oneness with God was David's greatest joy. In Psalm 17, which is really a prayer, he exclaims, "But as for me, my contentment is not in wealth but in seeing you and knowing all is well between us" (v. 15 LB). I love that. Isn't it a great feeling to know all is well between us and our best friend?

David found that Two-way Prayer was no fad or passing spiritual gimmick. He had made a dynamic discovery that constantly worked for him even in his old age. In Psalm 71 he says, "Now that I am old and gray . . . I will keep on expecting you to help me. I praise you more and more" (vv. 18, 14 LB). David writes of God's response to him in prayer. God helps him. He appears to him, instructs him, and shows his sensitivity and love.

"Sensitivity and love" is the very meaning of God's beautiful name in the Old Testament. God was originally called "Yahweh" in ancient times. The concept of God's being "kind and sensitive" is important when entering into a Two-way Prayer experience.

If God were not kind and loving, we'd be afraid to approach him. We wouldn't desire his nearness.

Jeremiah, an Old Testament prophet, found it rather exciting to approach God. Of Jeremiah's response from God in Two-way Prayer, we read, "The Lord, the Maker of heaven and earth—Jehovah is his name, says this: 'Ask me and I will tell you some remarkable secrets about what is going to happen here' " (Jer. 33:2, 3 LB).

It seems God wants us to ask him for advice. If he tells us to ask, it is reasonable to expect he will answer. He answers in many ways, but his verbal answers are stimulating. His thoughts have the pristine quality of love and truth as he makes himself available to us. He wants us to listen. *Listening* then, *is the fourth step* of Two-way Prayer.

Simple but not easy, the rewards of Two-way Prayer become treasured moments with God that the secular world cannot give or take away. The four basic steps are: one, *stop and let go* of muscular and mental tension; two, *look within ourselves* for negative emotions that need to be given to God. Three, *love God* and his majesty, thinking of his love and faithfulness for us; and, four, *listen* in silence and practice. God speaks. We need to have faith he will speak to us. STOP! LOOK! LOVE! LISTEN!

# 2

# *The Power of Your Inner World*

When we finally learn, as Rebecca, David, Jeremiah, and Isaiah did, to ask God, he does tell us remarkable things. Some of them are remarkable in their simplicity—like finding the route book. Some of them are dramatic—like a new business idea. All of the answers show God's loving sensitive care and desire to be our Friend. God will speak to us about our most basic need as he did to the businessman, the mother, and the minister.

The Lord has no favorites. He loves us all the same. He loves us as much as he loved Rebecca and David, who knew how to keep all the component parts of Two-way Prayer in proper balance.

Our physical bodies have component parts like an intricate machine. Intricate machines need to be understood to make them work properly. When something goes wrong, someone who thoroughly understands the machine can detect where the mechanism needs repair. Many times a minor adjustment makes the machine run smoothly again. To better comprehend prayer (what makes it work, what hinders its effect), we need to understand a little about the part of us that prays. This part is so carefully and precisely constructed that it baffles the most brilliant scientist. I am speaking of the magnificent human mind, splendid in its structure, potent and powerful in its function. Our minds contain hundreds of thousands of tiny brain cells in constant communication with each other. These are our personal inter-communication center to God. Let's consider this fascinating subject.

The desire to understand the mind and its function is as ancient as man and as modern as the computer. Now the curtain of intrigue and wonder is being drawn aside as a result of exciting discoveries in medical research. The more we explore, the more we learn about the God who designed our minds, and our inner as well as our outer world.

## How Do We Understand the Mind?

Until recently there were few objective or cognitive devices to measure our inner world. For about forty-five years technology has used the electro-encephalograph machine (the EEG) to register changes in brain activity and record them on polygraph paper. When turned on, the EEG machine, through electrodes placed on specific areas of the head, detects the slightest change in brain activity. Doctors have diagnosed such diseases as brain tumors or brain tissue damage through the changes in the EEG tracings. With the use of the EEG, researchers have done further studies of the brain during sleep, stress, confusion, peace, euphoria, and daydreams. The amazing result of this new knowledge has brought closer agreement and understanding among the three great disciplines pertaining to the total man: medicine, psychology, and theology.

Another device used in research to help us understand the mind is the biofeedback machine. The light-weight biofeedback machine, which is small enough to carry, is a high-powered detective device. Used extensively today, this machine has detected many psychological, medical, and spiritual problems.

## How Does the Mind Affect the Body?

One of the most striking discoveries of this research has been the language of the skin. It is possible to strap two small metal plates—electrodes—to the tips of the fingers. The biofeedback machine is so sensitive to the chemical changes on the skin that it will register even the slightest variation. Whatever the mind is thinking affects every cell in the body and the very chemistry of the skin.

As we change our thoughts, we change, ever so minutely, our skin chemistry. If our thoughts are hostile and tense, the machine registers the degree of tension. Then if we decide to change our thoughts to calm and peaceful ones, the indicator registers the message, reflecting the change sent from brain to skin. Amazingly perceptive, the biofeedback machine responds not only to our conscious, but to our unconscious thoughts or fears and resentments as well.

Many physical illnesses are linked to mental tension. Once the biofeedback machine has identified a tension-related physical or mental illness, Dr. Barbara Brown, a biomedical researcher at the University of California, trains her subject to break the tension cycle. The biofeedback training has been marvelously effective in curing migraine headaches, lowering blood pressure, curing ulcers, colitis, and other tension-related diseases. With the right instruments we finally know what God has told us all along (the mind controls the total well-being). "As (a man) thinketh . . . so is he" (Prov. 23:7). This fragile three-and-one-half-pound brain is the God-created instrument that can control man and his world.

### What Are the Four Patterns of the Brain?

These studies have led us to new insights into God's command to "be still." In reading the electrical impulses from the brain traced by the EEG, scientists have identified four different brain patterns, each sending its distinct path across the polygraph. These patterns correspond to activity in our waking and sleeping moments, under hypnosis, and during meditative moods. Scientists have labeled each characteristic pattern, beta, delta, theta, and alpha.

While we are in the waking or beta state, the EEG record is as personal to us as our fingerprints. While in beta, we may have a feeling of alertness and active thinking—or of surprise and excitement. Also tense negative feelings, such as fear, anger or worry, will register the high frequency beta waves. If our feelings are intense, there is a high beta index, meaning there is a higher concentration of beta waves.

When we lie down at night, our marvelous body processes

send thousands of signals to the obedient cells of our inner world that we desire sleep. Then we slip into the delta brain rhythm. This tremendously complex procedure of moving from the awake stage to sleep still puzzles medical science. Yet how beautifully God has designed us to slip into the sleeping state and out again with ease. In the morning we awaken as the gentle light of dawn brushes across our faces. We have been ushered safely and comfortably from our inner world and the subconscious to the outer conscious world—from the delta state of unawareness to the beta, or awake state. During the night we had been shut off to our incredible inner selves. During these hours of unawareness, God was healing our emotions and restoring mind, body, and soul. We awake refreshed.

Did you ever wake up in the stillness of the night and listen to the world? Most of its commotion and noise has ceased. There's a softness about the night that has a beauty of its own. With God's love and protection hovering around us, our thoughts may have been turned heavenward. Like David, we learn it is a marvelous time to pray. Many Christians have told of creative experiences while talking to God at night. One woman said, "I prayed and asked God what theme I could use to decorate for the mother-daughter banquet. Almost instantly there was a stream of ideas!" Another mother told me, "I was praying for my children during the night, and the thought came to me to check on how well my son was doing his homework. When I followed through on that inspiration, I found he had been neglecting it so badly he was headed for failure." A teenager said, "I woke up in the middle of the night and prayed because I was so nervous about the cheerleading tryouts. Something really neat happened! It was as if God himself said, 'Fear not, I am with thee.' After that I thought, *I want to be a cheerleader really bad, but if I don't make it, God is still with me . . . and my world won't fall apart!*"

## What Is the Alpha State?

Inspiration, instruction, comfort . . . treasures in the night! Are these treasures only for the night? No! They are available to us any time we need them. Nevertheless, since creative answers

| BRAIN WAVES | EXPERIENCES Physical and Emotional | GRAPH OF BRAIN WAVES |
|---|---|---|
| BETA 14 to 30 cycles per second | AWAKE STATE fully alert physical activity excitement fear tension anxiety | |
| ALPHA 8 to 13 cycles per second | PRE-DROWSINESS passive awareness composure pleasant mood deep relaxation of mind and body numbness of body | |
| THETA 4 to 7 cycles per second | DROWSINESS deep tranquility euphoric mood very deep relaxation often unconscious | |
| DELTA .05 to 3.5 cycles per second | DEEP SLEEP STATE total unawareness unconsciousness sleep | |

## FOUR BRAIN WAVE STATES

often come to us during our prayer at night, just as David's experiences did, let's take a look at what happens to the mind at a time like that.

If we were to apply the EEG device to examine the inner world, we would observe a person's mind flowing from delta (which has a low frequency brain wave) to theta and alpha. The diagram on the next page shows that the theta state also has a low electrical brain wave frequency. When one enters this state of mind, he feels drowsy and deeply relaxed. Sometimes the mind forms images, and what we call daydreaming takes place. It's a pleasant, tranquil mood. During such a time of peace and calm, the brain rhythms may show a burst of alpha waves.

Exciting and beautiful things happen during the alpha state. Research in alphagenics by Dr. Anthony Zaffuto has indicated that while in Alpha a person is capable of accelerated learning, healing of tension-related illnesses, increased creativity, memory improvement, and increased sensitivity to other peoples' needs and thoughts.[1]

Just as we all have beta, delta, and theta states, we also have alpha waves. The alpha brain wave level is entered as we move from the awake, alert or tense beta state to a level of physical and mental relaxation. Or we move into alpha if we are sleeping and gradually wake up but maintain a relaxed and peaceful mood. If we lie in bed with eyes closed, fully awake yet unaware of any physical and emotional distractions, we probably register a high alpha index. When the mind is still so that the incessant echoing of thoughts has ceased, one is beautifully prepared to enter into Two-way Prayer.

Though a sixteenth century monk didn't know about the alpha index, he did know about prayer. He devoted his life to the study of prayer and came to this conclusion: "The quiet that nature ordains before sleep is ordained by the devout soul for prayer." [2]

*How Does God Speak in the Stillness?*

When we learn how to still our minds, we will hear God. R. G. LeTourneau was taking an airplane trip with Napoleon

Hill. Soon after the pilot took off, Mr. LeTourneau fell asleep. In about thirty minutes Napoleon Hill saw him take a little notebook from his pocket and write several lines on it. After the plane landed, Napoleon Hill asked Mr. LeTourneau if he remembered writing in his notebook.

"Why no!" exclaimed Mr. LeTourneau. He immediately pulled the notebook from his pocket and looked at it. He said, "Here it is! I've been looking for this for several months! Here's the answer to a problem that has kept me from completing a machine we are working on!" [3]

The answer came to him in the stillness just as he was dozing off to sleep. Sometimes the answers come during sleep. God can speak when the ego of the conscious mind is in neutral gear.

David speaks of this quietness—no thoughts, no imagery— yet a keen awareness of God. He says, "I stand silently before the Lord . . . why then should I be tense with fear when trouble comes?" (Ps. 62:2 LB), and later, "Oh, God in Zion, we wait before you in silent praise" (Ps. 65:1 LB). When we do wait silently, we give God time to speak. This stage is simple; but it is not easy.

One of the hazards of this kind of prayer keeps it from being easy. When we reach the point of relaxation as in alpha, we are quite close to delta which is sleep. Some students say, "I think, instead of praying, I went to sleep." If this happens, there are techniques to help us stay awake. Sitting up instead of lying down will help. Or you can tell yourself ahead of time that you will not go to sleep and that you will focus on the alpha state. Despite our best efforts, if we still go to sleep, we won't despair. God knows we needed the sleep more than we needed the prayer.

*Do We Have an Avenue to God's Thoughts?*

Once a person trains himself to be sensitive to the thoughts of God, he may not need to get into deep relaxation to carry on a dialogue with Christ. Many great spiritual leaders in our time have a running conversation with God throughout the day.

I have known Joyce Landorf for nearly fifteen years. This gifted author, speaker, singer, and friend often tells her audiences something like this: "And so, God told me I should send my sister some money. As a result of doing it, my sister shared with me a desperate need." Joyce told me that when she invites inquiries from her audiences, the most commonly asked question is, "Do you actually hear God's voice when you say 'God told me'?" No, Joyce hears God's thoughts. She has grown sensitive to his direction through wanting it and by obeying it. In chapter 7 we will explain specifically how to do this.

The late Dr. Henrietta Mears, founder of Forest Home Christian Conference Center in California, was visiting our home when she said, "God told me this morning he wanted us to build a larger dining hall at the center. I said, 'O.K. Lord, but where should we put it?' He said, 'Right next to the book store.' I said, 'But we don't have the money.' He said, 'The money will be there.'" All who knew this great woman of God recognize that she talked about God as a personal friend. She had constant dialogue with Christ and talked with him while riding in a car, working in the house, or walking to the sanctuary.

Dr. Mears' accomplishments, including the founding of Gospel Light Publishing House, are dynamic witnesses of God's guidance in her life. Nevertheless, there is a danger in this practice. Some people may do this and not be receiving God's thoughts, but rather their own. They simply talk to themselves. Is there a way to determine what are God's thoughts and what are our own? Yes. A thorough understanding of Two-way Prayer and its dangers will prevent us from getting into trouble with it. Two-way Prayer is a sensitive technique that needs to be respected. It ought not be entered into casually or carelessly.

## Is There a Way to Discern God's Thoughts?

As we take our first toddling steps in the journey toward a powerful and creative prayer experience, we must learn to distinguish between a self-inspired thought and a God-inspired thought. We certainly want to avoid the ways that seem right but cause destruction of self or our fellowmen. "There is a way which seemeth right unto a man, but the end thereof are the ways of death" (Prov. 14:12). Nevertheless, we can test our thoughts against three general principles: 1) Do they inspire wisdom and insight? 2) Do they inspire virtue? 3) Do they inspire love?

1) Do they inspire wisdom and insight that has:
    a) no ulterior motives?
    b) no strife?
    c) respect and consideration?
    d) no confusion?
2) Do they inspire virtue such as:
    a) common sense?
    b) endurance (physical and mental)?
    c) moderation?
    d) justice to mankind?
    e) faith in God?
    f) hope that it is attainable?
    g) love of giving to others?
3) Do they inspire love for:
    a) God?
    b) yourself?
    c) others?

## *What Is the Test of a Divine Creative Thought?*

The kind of inspiration that comes from God is not earthly, sensual or vindictive. Nor is it possessive or egocentric. These are traps of the adamic nature and we must be discerning of any form of subtlety. It is well for the student of prayer to pray for the gift of discernment. Some thoughts that come to us are of a totally creative nature. To distinguish if a creative idea is from God or self we can test it against four questions:

1) Does it agree with the Bible?
2) Will it honor God?
3) Will it be good for mankind?
4) Has it ever been done before?

The Scriptures give us authority that has stood the test of time. James 3:17 tells us: "But the wisdom that is from above is first pure, then peaceable, gentle, and easy to be entreated, full of mercy and good fruits, without partiality, and without hypocrisy."

Sometimes the information we receive in Two-way Prayer is of a prophetic nature. Most of the time God gives the insight for our own personal benefit; for instance, to prepare us emotionally for a critical incident; or to stand confidently with a friend who is wavering, lending poise and strength. Prophetic knowledge helps us guide our intimate families through times of uncertainty. Nevertheless, as powerful and beautiful as these plans of God are, it is his special love and grace that causes him to share his plans with us. We must take great care not to exploit and misuse these treasured messages.

The ego is extremely vulnerable at these times. For the most part, prophetic thoughts are best kept in the intimate communication between the receiver and God. As did Mary, the espoused wife of Joseph, when the angel told her she was going to give birth to the Messiah, we should keep "these things" and ponder them in our heart (Luke 2:19). Unless we are very sure we are to share a prophetic inspiration, it is best to keep it as a private thought between God and ourselves. If in doubt, we can ask God if we should share it, taking special notice of our own motivation.

To understand the devious ways of the "old nature" and its interference in Two-way Prayer, it is helpful to understand the levels of the mind. We will look at this in detail in the next chapter.

# 3

# *The Anatomy of Prayer*

When I was a little girl in Michigan, one of the highlights of my week was a trip to my uncle's farm in the western part of the state. I remember leaving Grand Rapids in our old Ford car, traveling down Chicago Drive to the Jenison grain mill. We made a right turn into Georgetown Township and on to Riveredge Farm. With six bouncing, enthusiastic kids in the car, my dad whistled all the way. He knew we couldn't wait to run in the corn field or to ride the cows.

As we grew older, we began to notice how hard Uncle Paul worked. We watched him cultivate, fertilize, and harvest. Yet the progress was slow. The work horses grew old and tired. The buildings needed paint. Through scrimping, he made a living, but that was all. In those days there was no way for us to understand why he had to work so hard. The crops didn't flourish the way they should have with extra help and tender, loving care, even though the farm had the lush, nourishing advantage of being next to a flowing river.

### *Gravel Gold Mine*

Our family grew up and we all moved away. When Uncle Paul died, the farm was sold back to its original owners, the Boynton family. They knew the farm was nonproductive because the ground was mostly gravel. Yet, up to that time technology hadn't developed a way to extract that certain type of gravel. It needed a special process before it could be prepared for sale.

One can ride through the neighboring towns such as Wyoming and Grandville and see any number of gravel pits. As a child,

I thought as did so many people, *Gravel is gravel! So why can't you dig it up, sell it, and get rich?*

Just the other day, I visited Mr. and Mrs. George Boynton who are still living on the farm. They explained that there are different kinds of gravel. Some consists of clean stones, easily extracted and sold. Then there is gravel mixed with clay which must be washed and separated. This was the kind of gravel on Uncle Paul's old farm. Little did he realize he was sitting on a gravel gold mine. Once technology brought understanding into a new process, Mr. Boynton could develop the Riverside Gravel Company. He purchased the equipment, extracted the gravel, and developed a thriving business.

I couldn't help remembering the many years Uncle Paul struggled to produce something out of the farm. It was a beautiful piece of land, running alongside the Grand River. It had to be productive! Actually, with tons of gravel beneath the crops, all the fertilizer and water ran through the land like a giant sieve. Trying to grow crops on that property was not using the land's real potential. God never intended it to be a farm. The natural law for that land was to be a gravel pit, not a corn field.

*Prayer Gold Mine*

To some people prayer is like Uncle Paul's corn field: they know it should be working, but it isn't. The people love God, they read the Bible, and they go to church. They believe in prayer, and they hear about other people praying—talking to God and God talking to them. Frankly, they are spiritually cultivated, spiritually irrigated, and spiritually seeded, and yet their prayer crop is not what they expected it to be. Up to this point in their lives, they have not been able to extract the vital experience with God that comes with Two-way Prayer. Technology such as biofeedback, EEG, GSR, and EMG, has now been developed which helps us understand the harmony between body, mind, and soul. It's this harmony which makes prayer potential dynamically effective.

We have said that body and mind are in constant communication. They are like inseparable Siamese twins. As the body relaxes, it induces the mind to relax. But what happens to the soul when the mind is still? The soul's expression, gentle and quiet in nature, then has beautiful communion with a sensitive, loving, powerful God. This expression is best heard by reaching the inner depths of one's being. The more deeply relaxed one becomes without going to sleep, the more quickly one reaches the very level of the mind where he can best commune with his heavenly Father.

## Six Levels of the Mind

Perhaps this process can be explained by imagining the mind to be made up of different layers. Some psychologists feel there may be many layers of the mind, but for practical prayer purposes, we'll talk about only six of them. Try to picture the mind as a firm round Spanish onion sliced in half. We can easily see the many layers of skin. The outer layer represents the first level of the mind which is the five senses; the second layer is the conscious mind; the third, the subconscious mind; the fourth is the superconscious mind; the fifth layer is the Christ-conscious and the sixth and innermost layer is the God-conscious mind. See figure on next page.

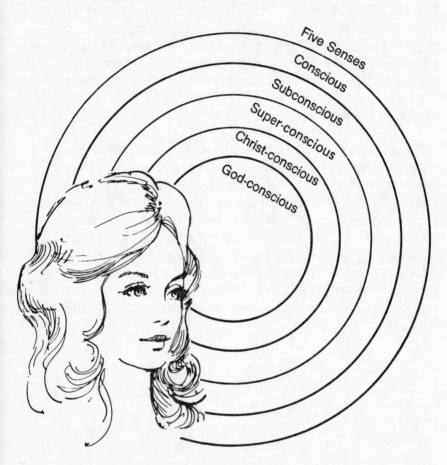

Five Senses
Conscious
Subconscious
Super-conscious
Christ-conscious
God-conscious

LEVELS OF THE MIND

## The Sensory Level and Our Outer World

Why do we call the mind a most splendid and remarkable machine? Everything we know or experience from our outer world has been transmitted and translated deep within our inner world. These experiences are discovered at the *first level* of our *five senses.* These senses—sight from our eyes, hearing from our ears, touch from the skin, taste from the tongue, and smell from the nose—become windows through which the outer, sensory world can enter our minds and become part of us.

We can experience pleasant sensations that live long in the memory. Think of walking into a quiet, elegant restaurant where we are graciously escorted to a table. We order a filet mignon. When the waiter brings the sizzling, grilled meat, the olfactory nerves which line the inner nose send messages to the brain. The complex ocular nerves in the eye send signals conveying that not only does the meat look delicious, but so does our companion. Candlelight casts its glow on the food and the people! The aroma of candles blends with the scent of steak; the nose and the eyes send pleasant messages to the brain. Our touch mechanism and taste buds signal that the succulent meat is tender and savory. Against the background of soft music and treasured conversation with a cherished friend, our auditory nerves become the antennae transporting pleasant sounds within the body.

## The Conscious Level and Our Decisions

All of these sensations go to *the second level, the conscious mind.* On this level we make our decisions. We say, "I like the taste of this steak." The conscious mind is the marvelous mechanism which separates man from lower forms of life. Within that level, man develops his logical cognitive thinking. His decision making and reasoning stem from the conscious mind.

This level is a wonderful and necessary part of mankind, but he must recognize its dangers. The conscious mind can get a person into deep trouble. Because it is devious and cunning, it cannot be totally trusted. The motives of the conscious mind must be examined constantly. One of the reasons it is dangerous is that it is in close communication with our five senses. The power of our senses can overwhelm the sensible logic of our conscious mind.

We might see a car we can't afford . . . but it looks so beautiful and feels so luxurious. Our logical thinking may warn us of pending disaster if we overspend. This warning is drowned out by the torrential impulses of our senses. The car is beautiful, quiet, luxurious to ride in. It looks, sounds, and feels good! After we give in to our sensual desires and buy the car, we find the car payments so high we have to push ourselves beyond healthy limits to get out of debt.

Our five senses are like five spoiled children constantly screaming for attention. Only the conscious mind can discipline these children and bring them under control in an act of the will. But an important thing to remember about the conscious mind is that it can twist the truth ever so subtly for selfish reasons.

### Subconscious Level and Our Memory Bank

Days, weeks, and years after that memorable dinner with the steak, candlelight, and good friend, we can relish and relive the experience. The conscious mind stores that information in *the third level, the subconscious.* The subconscious is our memory bank. Through the awesome wonder of our memory bank, every impression of that evening has been recorded in the minutest detail. The very next time someone asks us if we would like a filet mignon, we say, "Yes." The decision comes as a result of a pleasant memory recalled from the subconscious. The subconscious, with split-second timing, sends a positive experience with filet mignon to the conscious mind and the decision is made to please the taste buds once more!

We make thousands of decisions every day. That is why we need the third level of the mind, the subconscious or unconscious, to help us recall experiences in making decisions. The memory bank does not know right from wrong. It does not think logically, nor does it make decisions. The subconscious mind believes everything it is told by the conscious mind. Every experience, good and bad, right or wrong, is recorded in the subconscious. The memories recorded with the strongest emotions are the most indelible. These memories make up 90 percent of the total personality.

The programming of the subconscious mind can be both harmful and beneficial to man. Bathed and pink-cheeked, a little tike toddles off to bed. An older brother or sister may be lurking around the corner. In the dark, and "just for fun," he jumps out and shouts, "Boooooo!" The unexpected and sudden loud noise in the dark registers through the ears and eyes to the conscious mind of the toddler. His conscious mind is abruptly startled by a new experience. The decision is made to let his entire body know that an emergency exists. The adrenal gland shoots adrenalin into the bloodstream for extra energy so that the toddler can either run—or stay and fight.

The terrifying experience took place in the dark. It was not meant to hurt the child but rather merely to tease him. Nevertheless, the experience was recorded by the subconscious that when it is dark, fearful things happen! From that moment on, when alone in the dark, the child is afraid. The subconscious mind is highly sensitive and vulnerable to suggestion.

There was an experiment done in the crowded tenement section of New York City after a preliminary experiment with white rats which illustrated the sensitivity of the subconscious mind to suggestion.

A few white rats played contentedly in a large cage with an exercise wheel and food. As more rats were added, the rats began to show signs of irritation. Still more rats were added. Conditions within the cage became unbearable for the animals. They grew aggressive and began to attack each other. They fought and finally began to gnaw and chew at the weaker ones, until they killed them. As the scientist began removing a number of rats daily from the cage, the behavior of the remaining animals returned to normal. Once again they had room to live and play happily. The rats needed a physical change to alter their behavior.

In the human situation where crowded tenants lived in one

room, an experiment in New York City was performed for several weeks and showed the ability of mental change to alter behavior. Half of the members in a one-room apartment remained the same, representing a control group. The other half were trained in a special technique of meditation. They were told to sit quietly, relax their bodies and close their eyes. With their eyes closed, they were told to imagine a quiet place where they could be alone and at peace. For twenty minutes, through the miracle of their minds, they could see themselves being transported to a troutstream, the French countryside, or a white sandy beach where they could bask in sunshine. The mind and body responded in every way as if they had actually been there. By the end of the experiment, their personalities were friendly, helpful, and happy, while the control group continued to show signs of neurotic behavior. The untrained group exhibited aggressive and irritable personalities. Angry and dissatisfied, they inappropriately attacked their fellowman.

Through other studies of the mind, we realize the power of the subconscious upon our personalities. If the little toddler thinks the darkness hurts him, he will carry that fear twenty-four hours a day. If a New York City tenant thinks he's been to a troutstream, his body and personality react accordingly. The subconscious mind's belief in everything it is told has a marked effect on the body. For the most part, we control what we are told by conscious interpretation of a given situation. Whether we interpret an incident negatively or positively is our powerful choice.

*The Superconscious Level and Our Genius Mind*

Within the subconscious mind we find another inner source of power. The diagram on the next page specifies that *the fourth level of the mind* is *the superconscious* or *the genius mind.* It is the source of creativity and a treasured storehouse of our abilities or talents. We all have a genius mind. It supplies us with an inner ability to do something with greater ease and efficiency than the average person. The Bible speaks of this ability as "gifts" or "talents." To understand how the stored talents are dispersed,

# Levels of the Mind

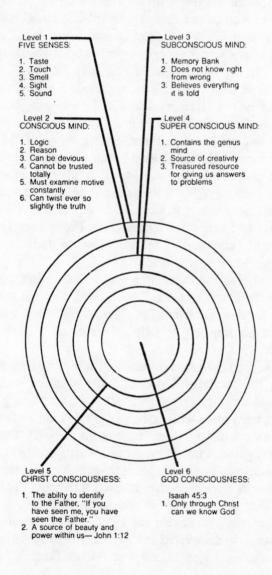

Level 1
FIVE SENSES:

1. Taste
2. Touch
3. Smell
4. Sight
5. Sound

Level 2
CONSCIOUS MIND:

1. Logic
2. Reason
3. Can be devious
4. Cannot be trusted
   totally
5. Must examine motive
   constantly
6. Can twist ever so
   slightly the truth

Level 3
SUBCONSCIOUS MIND:

1. Memory Bank
2. Does not know right
   from wrong
3. Believes everything
   it is told

Level 4
SUPER CONSCIOUS MIND:

1. Contains the genius
   mind
2. Source of creativity
3. Treasured resource
   for giving us answers
   to problems

Level 5
CHRIST CONSCIOUSNESS:

1. The ability to identify
   to the Father, "If you
   have seen me, you have
   seen the Father."
2. A source of beauty and
   power within us— John 1:12

Level 6
GOD CONSCIOUSNESS:

Isaiah 45:3
1. Only through Christ
   can we know God

picture an imaginary spout that regulates the flow of ideas. If this spout could be directed to the genius level of the mind and the spigot opened, there would be an abundant flow of ideas in a given segment of creative power. What opens the spigot? Some feel it opens when we quiet the first three levels during Two-way Prayer, or sometimes through an intense emotional crisis.

My friend, Joyce Landorf, tells of an intense emotional struggle that may have been a peak experience in her creative and spiritual development. In her book, *Joyce, I Feel Like I Know You . . .* , she tells about an overwhelming experience of loneliness she had at the age of eleven. Her mother and father were both gone when she came home from school one day. She needed someone to talk with but no one was there. Sitting down at the piano, she tried to practice. Her depression became worse as her feelings of loneliness increased. She continued to play some old-time hymns rather passively. " . . . then the strangest thing happened. I was aware that I was not alone. God's presence filled every available space and at first it frightened me. Pretty soon I stopped playing, began to cry (my life motto: 'When in doubt, cry') and finally said out loud, 'Lord, is that You?'

"As I recall, He didn't answer me; but it didn't matter. I knew it was the Spirit of God, He was real, and He was there with me." [1] Joyce knew from that time on that God was going to use her in his ministry to help others come to love and to know Christ.

Joyce has tapped the genius level of her mind in many different places. Like the facets of a diamond she sparkles with many talents. The talents are there. Her gifted piano playing, lovely singing voice, witty and picturesque way of speaking, or the ability to write books could have been directed in any way she chose. She could have gained fame in the secular world, or world renown in the Christian community, depending on her inner orientation. Untold thousands have been strengthened spiritually because she chose to use her talents to tell others about Christ.

On the other hand, we have many geniuses in the secular world who have obviously discovered some facet of their genius mind— people with extraordinary talents like Albert Einstein, Ludwig von Beethoven, Madame Curie, Dr. Michael De Bakey, the famous heart surgeon, and Barbara Jordan, the politician. These are dramatic examples. Some people are especially gifted with economic or secretarial skills. Others are expert at car repairing, sewing or food preparation. A woman in our church, Phyllis Stulp, makes exquisite wedding cakes. She sews the bride's dress and all the attendants' dresses. All this she accomplishes with joy and ease. I would become mentally deranged if I tackled such as assignment. Perhaps future research in the alpha or theta states will give us exciting insights into the mystery of the genius mind.

## Christ-consciousness Level and Healing

Although simple meditative techniques can take a person to the genius mind, only prayer can take a person beyond. The next two levels, Christ-consciousness and God-consciousness, are pure gold to the inner personality. *The fifth level, the Christ-conscious mind,* is the healing ointment for troubled psyches, the cure for all loneliness, the source of creative answers to problems, and the very heart of vibrant, confident living. Christ-discernment, Christ-awareness or Christ-consciousness, whatever we choose to call it, is the ability within every man, woman, and child to perceive Jesus Christ, to identify and to receive him. Only by going through the Christ-conscious level of the mind can we know the Father through *the sixth level of the mind* called *God-consciousness.*

## God-consciousness Level and Harmony with God

By the time we have reached the sixth level of the mind in the process called Two-way Prayer, we have broken through the tension-hardened layers with our imaginary spigot. Our inner being becomes compatible to and at harmony with God. This is the structure of the mind. I'm not speaking of the brain. The mind takes in much more than the brain. Some scientists believe these levels of the mind are found in every cell of the body.

Each cell has a complicated communication system with one another and with God. But how are these levels affected in prayer?

## Moving through the Levels into Two-way Prayer

As our bodies become still, it is easy to withdraw from the outer sensory world simply by closing our eyes. As we enter our inner world, we leave our five senses on automatic pilot! They are functioning efficiently, but our minds are not drawn out to them. Our senses become keenly aware of the environment in case of danger or necessity.

We now slip into the inner closet that Christ talked about in Matthew 6:6. While we quiet our muscles, our conscious minds may still be busy thinking. We cannot concentrate in our prayer because our thoughts flit from subject to subject. Our feelings may be vague and unfocused. Research has taught us that the mind cannot think of two things at once. Thus, whispering in our stream of consciousness a word or phrase repetitiously, will discourage our busy minds from fragmented thoughts. As our thoughts become less active and our arms and legs feel light, we move toward the inner levels of the mind.

Leaving the conscious mind, we enter the subconscious, the memory bank. This is a good time to contemplate any harbored negative emotions or guilt for wrongdoing, to search for unresolved fears and resentments. When a fear comes to mind, we give it to Christ. Next, we search for any resentments. Has anyone done something offensive to us which we have not forgiven? After we ask God to forgive our resentment, we have to forgive ourselves. We have to see ourselves with no resentment toward that person—replacing the resentment with love and forgiveness. This is not easy to do—but the rewards are liberating—to be free from the self-induced chains of resentment!

We learn the power and beauty of forgiving the other person without his asking for it. It's the kind of forgiveness Christ demonstrated on the cross when he said, "Father, forgive them for they know not what they do." The slightest negative emotion, conscious or subconscious, can cause tension and bring discord between the levels of the mind. As we get rid of our negative emotions, the mind becomes more and more relaxed. With mental relaxation, we go into the deeper levels of the mind. The body's reaction, which results from a peaceful state of mind, can be demonstrated on the biofeedback machine.

Next, we turn our thoughts to God's love for us. After David's soul-searching prayer, he thought about God's love. This is important. It is good to remain silent in the mighty presence of God for a few moments. Feeling his love, we let him feel ours. We feel oneness with him, and we sense his understanding. There is a sense of belonging to him. When we have finished our prayer, we whisper quietly in our thoughts, "Thank You, Father," three times. This brings us gently back through all the levels of the mind to our sensory world. As we open our eyes we notice how composed and poised we feel.

The art of true prayer is worthy of the time and energy invested in studying all of its intricacies. Just as we develop skills in everything else, we need also to develop skill in prayer.

# 4

# *The Power of the Mind and the Power of Two-way Prayer*

How we limit God by not utilizing the power he has given us. The power of the mind is compared to a laser beam. Penetrating stone and steel, the laser beam has highly amplified electromagnetic frequencies. A professor from San Jose State College found from his research that the human mind is seventeen times more powerful than the laser beam! We are powerful people. When we and God get together, there is no limitation on what we can do! "The effectual fervent prayer of a righteous man availeth much" (James 5:16) is the great biblical understatement. It should have been translated, "The effectual fervent prayer of a righteous man availeth enormous, *dynamic* things!"

*Prayer Power Is Visual*

Prayer power is mind power that is God-centered or God-directed. Prayer has a significant effect on other people. For centuries Christians have testified of the power of prayer, but not until recently did we know how visually prayer could be demonstrated.

I've been told of a group of students who sat in a research lab in one of the leading California universities. One student was instructed to think of someone else in the room. A specially developed camera with highly sensitized film took a picture of the room. When the film was developed, the picture showed a sheer cloudy substance from the head of the student to the very one he was thinking about. If the electrical emissions from our

54

brains can be directed at will to a place we think of, what effect do God-centered thoughts have on those we think about?

Physicist Dr. J. E. Zimmerman has developed a brain wave device that can pick up the magnetic emissions from the brain of a student without touching him. In an annual report to Congress last year, researchers of three U.S. laboratories reported they have learned to tell, with 90 percent accuracy, whether a person is:

- puzzled
- certain and decisive
- alert
- observing colors or
- daydreaming

This test tells us specific thought patterns can be picked up by sensitive objective devices. How do these God-centered thoughts affect those to whom we direct them? Will science tell us all in time how truly effective prayer is? Or will we have to wait until some future date when we get to heaven and have God tell us? I sometimes read Revelation 7:17, "And God shall wipe away all tears from their eyes," and wonder, "Will my tears be there because I suddenly become aware of the power of prayer . . . and I didn't use it more!"

The power of prayer was well known to Alexis Carrel. Dr. Carrel was a French surgeon and biologist who proved that living tissues could survive apart from their organs if properly nourished. This contribution was the forerunner to modern-day organ transplants. In 1912 he won the Nobel Prize for his work in blood vessel surgery. One of the world's foremost scientists speaking to a generation familiar with thermonuclear power, Dr. Carrel said, "The most powerful form of energy one can generate is prayer. Prayer like radium is luminous and a self-generating form of energy." Prayer is more powerful than mechanical, electronic or even atomic energy.

*A Ten Million Dollar Prayer*

An instance of such prayer power began early one Saturday in February, 1976. The sky was translucent blue. The sun bounced off the hoods of the cars traveling the freeway. In the distance I could see a lofty cross towering over a restless, bustling southern California city. I knew it wouldn't be long before I would be entering the church where I was to meet the senior pastor.

Silently I prayed that God would do something significant in the hours to follow. I felt his presence as I rode the elevator to the twelfth floor and took a seat in the waiting room of the pastor's office. The study door opened, and there stood a tall gentleman, shoulders back, head held high. His broad grin and friendly hello showed no signs of the enormous pressure he must bear as the pastor of a congregation of 12,000 people.

He was eager to hear about Two-way Prayer. His desire to learn something new and wonderful about God was almost boyish. There was an innocence, an openness about him that I found refreshing. With quiet enthusiasm he shared his thoughts on prayer, and I shared mine. Innately he knew the concepts of Two-way Prayer as I defined them. He nodded and smiled. After four hours of explaining the biblical principles, I told him that Two-way Prayer had to be experienced to be appreciated. With a total lack of arrogance, he was willing for me to lead him in an exercise of Two-way Prayer.

"That was a beautiful experience," he said at the close of the exercise. We spent the next few moments in a quiet discussion of God's wondrous love in prayer. When we admitted to each other that God not only does meet our needs, but loves to give us our deepest wishes, his voice deepened with concern. "We need more room. There are so many people having to stand through Sunday services—some having to sit on the grass outside; some turning around and going back home. Oh, the hurt, the pain I see! I know what we could do for them." The deepest need on his heart at that point was for the seemingly impossible sum of ten million dollars to build a sanctuary to seat more people.

At that moment, I promised myself and God that I would spend time every day praying that this church would have the ten million dollars soon. I knew the pastor's motive was pure, the need was urgent, and God could do it!

I remember the joy of praying for about forty-five minutes in the early morning hours. For about six or seven weeks I prayed every day. One morning God said to me, "Perky, I have heard your prayers for the ten million dollars for the new sanctuary. I will provide it, only don't think it will come about because of the multitude of your words!"

I said, "O.K., Lord. You mean I don't have to pray about it anymore?"

"That's right," was the answer. It was one of those times that the Lord told me: "You've prayed long enough!"

Just before Easter that spring, Arvella, the pastor's wife, called me.

"Have you heard?" she asked. "We received a million-dollar gift as a direct result of Two-way Prayer." Nearly two weeks later an assistant pastor's wife told me the church had received its second million-dollar gift. By early summer four million dollars had been donated.

Dr. Robert Schuller's testimony is public that the Lord, through Two-way Prayer, guided him to the people and to the plans he wanted for his sanctuary. Without arrogance, he followed God's gentle nudgings. In less than eighteen months before the ground-breaking, God had provided the entire ten million dollars to finance his place of worship in Garden Grove, California.

The building will have ten thousand windows to reflect God's love. The pastor prayed, "God, make me a window to see you clearly and reflect Christ's love to others." This answer to Two-way Prayer has to stand as a monument before man. God must have wanted his symbol of love to be fully paid for so that he provided the total of ten million dollars before the building program began. God's answer in Two-way Prayer was complete and dramatic.

## Secret of Serenity

Dr. Robert Schuller, the pastor of the Garden Grove Drive-in Church in California, has learned to touch the heart of God. He has learned to be successful in prayer without being arrogant in his mind. A man marvelously at peace with himself, God, and his fellowman, Dr. Schuller preached a series of sermons on Two-way Prayer. The first in the series was "The Secret of Serenity." He listed seven secrets to finding mental, physical, and spiritual harmony in prayer:

1) *Neutralize*—Throw self-will gears into neutral. Go into prayer without any preconceived ideas or opinions. Tell God you have everything to learn. Neutralize your prejudices. Get rid of fixed and unbending opinions about things and people.

2) *Harmonize*—Prayer is not a solo. It is a duet in harmony with God. The harmony begins when you think his name.

3) *Sterilize*—Sterilize your thinking by getting rid of toxic negative emotions. Give your fears and resentments to God. As you get rid of your grudges, you will throw open the door to the superconscious mind to hear clearly the thoughts from God. "Heal the grudge and you'll feel God's nudge," he said.

4) *Tranquilize*—A sixteenth century monk said, "The act of contemplation is the act of love for God." We bring our outer and inner worlds into balance as we enter the alpha state. Then the love thoughts of God will tranquilize our entire person.

5) *Visualize*—In the presence of God visualize success, courage, poise or Christ Jesus. Visualize a scripture portion such as Psalm 23 or a parable.

6) *Possibilitize*—Plan your dream. See it happen.

7) *Actualize*—The final step in Two-way Prayer is doing what you and God have agreed to do. It is the physical act of carrying out his best advice for you.

## The Power for Abundant Living

The stages of relaxation during a Two-way Prayer exercise have specific mental, physical, and spiritual feelings. The chart on the next page helps us detect what stage we're experiencing. We may not have a machine that tells us what brain wave pattern we're producing; yet it is possible to become sensitive to our bodily feelings and mental state which corresponds to our prayer feelings. When David was too upset to pray, he was extremely

# STAGES OF PRAYER

| | Mental Feelings | Physical Feelings | Prayer Feelings |
|---|---|---|---|
| **Beta** | Wide awake | Extreme tension | Too upset to pray |
| | Excitement | Up-tight | Feel God is not listening |
| | Frustration | Very active | Feel God is far away |
| | Alert | Accelerated motions | One-way prayer |
| | Mind active | Metabolism high | One-way prayer |
| | Normal thoughts | Less stressful | One-way prayer |
| | Relaxing thoughts | Muscles loosening | Thinking of a tranquil place |
| **Alpha** | Thoughts quieting | Five senses on automatic pilot | Enjoy a beautiful place |
| | Moments of stillness | Numb, quiet | Silent praise |
| | Withdraw into inner world | Deep relaxation | Feelings of oneness with God |
| | Mind totally aware of inner world | Floating feeling | Communing with God—Moments of creative thoughts |
| **Theta** | Drowsiness | Unaware | Releasing negative emotions |
| | Visualizing | Unaware | Speaking to Christ and listening |
| | Unconscious | Unconscious | |
| **Delta** | Deep sleep | Unconscious | Letting Christ speak through the images of your dreams—Healing emotions—Creative answers—in dreams |

tense because he was afraid for his life; he felt God was far away. He must have been producing a high beta index. When we become too upset to pray, Romans 8:26 is a comfort: "Likewise the Spirit also helpeth our infirmities: for we know not what we should pray for as we ought; but the Spirit itself maketh intercession for us with groanings which cannot be uttered."

When the mind is alert and active, and the metabolism high, we can appropriately make use of the first three forms of prayer—praise, petition, and intercession. These one-way prayers are powerful and effective. But to learn to know God in close communion we should loosen our muscles and relax our thoughts, as we move from the beta to alpha state. But a check on our mental and physical feeling can aid our prayer life. Thinking of a tranquil or beautiful place in nature automatically soothes and quiets the tense mind. At the same time, this helps us move from our sensory level of the mind, through the conscious and subconscious levels. The body begins to feel light and easy and, perhaps, we even have a floating, numb feeling so that we aren't conscious of the chair in which we're sitting. This is an excellent indication that we are ready for a meaningful communion with God in Two-way Prayer. It is this exquisite experience that furnishes us with spiritual refreshment, physical restoration, and mental realignment.

A busy mother can rest physically, perform her God-given priestly duty of interceding for her children, and collect her thoughts before the Lord for his approval or rearrangement.

A pressured businessman can gain creative answers to personnel problems with God's direction. A college student can learn to clear his mind and let God enhance the learning process by erasing the impediments, thus bringing order out of confusion. A widow can walk and talk with the Man from Galilee, bringing relief from her intense loneliness.

Success in life and success in Two-way Prayer are companions. The learning principles for each are the same. Life becomes an adventure with God. It's no wonder we have this urge to live with him.

# 5

# *The Urge to Live with God*

Getting to know God is an achievement just as getting to know another person is an achievement. When two people fall in love they become enthralled with the discovery of one another. There is such delight and strong feeling of fellowship in each others' presence that they carve out the time to be together. It seems the more one gets to know the other person, the more one learns about himself. Over a period of time the things they like together are the things they talk about, and so their friendship grows and love flourishes.

There are three levels of relationship man can have with God. First, he may merely believe in God. That's not getting very far. The devils believe and tremble. Secondly, he may be acquainted with God. That's not a very close relationship either. We are acquainted with many people, yet we still don't know them well. Thirdly, one may be a friend of God. In other words, he loves God and is not afraid of God. His conscience toward God is clear. It is this third level that is really vital. How can this stage be achieved? How do we become a friend of God? How do we live with God?

## *Becoming God's Friend in Two-way Prayer*

Achieving the third level can be easy. God becomes our friend simply as we ask him. It has been an exciting thing for me to watch God become a Friend to my students.

A few people who come to the Two-way Prayer seminar have to learn first to become a friend of God. They believe in God. They are well acquainted with his ways for they know the Scrip-

61

tures well. But they have never told him they wanted him to be part of their lives.

## Becoming God's Friend

About twenty of the loveliest and most noble women I have ever seen came to a seminar for pastors' wives. I knew them all. I had watched their gentle Christlike patience endure the greatest tenacity test of any woman, that of sharing their God-fearing husbands with hundreds of people on a daily basis—year in and year out. They all deserved a medal of honor for holding their families together.

As I lectured them, I looked in each face and felt an enormous love. Several wives deserved two medals! They had been daughters of parents who were in the ministry, thus sharing the attention of mothers and fathers with the community as well.

Such was the case with Ann. I had known her even as a teenager. Her parents managed a Christian Retreat Center. Her boy friend had decided to become a minister during the week my husband directed church camp there. In later years they married and became established in an exciting church. Now she was in the group. Beginning to lead them in a Two-way Prayer experience, I told them to "close your eyes and go through the deep breathing exercises, four times." When they became physically relaxed, and mentally still, I told them to imagine a beautiful place. Thinking of a beautiful place of quiet and peacefulness helps the mind become tranquil. Then I said, "Imagine someone in the distance coming toward you. As he gets closer, notice that it is Jesus." A tear slid down Ann's cheek. I continued. Another tear, then another. I noticed her face becoming blotchy and her nose turning red. I knew she was muffling her sobs. The others sat quietly and peacefully. Ann opened her eyes and reached into her purse for a handkerchief. Then she left the room.

After the session I asked, "Ann, what happened?"

"You told us to visualize a quiet place," she said. "I did. I imagined myself sitting on a hill at my parents' retreat center.

Not far away was a natural cave with a large stone alongside. It depicts Christ's tomb and I loved going there as a child. We used it for Easter sunrise services.

"Then you said, 'Now, look up and see Jesus coming to you.' Perky, I waited for him to come out of the tomb. Something inside me told me he had to come out of the tomb—but he didn't come. He didn't come. I waited. No Jesus!" She was holding the damp crumpled handkerchief to her runny nose.

I leaned close and lowered my voice, "Ann, does Jesus seem real to you?"

She shook her head no.

"Does he seem alive in your life?" Again, no.

"Do you want him to be your Friend . . . alive and real?" She nodded yes.

"Have you ever asked him to be your Friend?"

Her eyes widened, her mouth dropped open. "No, I guess I never really did ask him! Perky, thank you! I've got to go now. I want to go home. I know just what I have to do!"

Nearly a year later she came to another seminar. During one of the coffee breaks, she made her way down the crowded aisle toward me.

"Perky," she said, "my life was totally changed that day. I've brought fifteen women from our church because they've seen the change in me."

What happened to Ann that made such a difference in her life? The doors of the fifth and sixth levels of her mind were flung open because she invited Christ to become alive in her life. Her identification with Christ was simultaneous with her awareness of God.

The Bible says, "As many as received him (Christ) to them gave he the power to become the sons of God" (John 1:12). Christ-consciousness, the fifth level, needs to be quickened before we can know God as our Friend. We cannot get to know God without knowing Christ. The Bible says no man has seen God the Father at any time. How can we know someone we can't see?

If I were to hold out my empty hand and say, "Do you see what I hold in my hand? It's invisible. Do you like it? Would you like to take it home and put it on your kitchen table? Do you want to become like it?" You'd answer, "I don't know. I can't see it!"

How can we know God if we can't see him? How do we know if we'd like him, or want to become like him?

But Jesus said in effect, "If you have seen me, you have seen the Father." Once we identify with Christ, we see God. We can know what Jesus was like by reading Matthew, Mark, Luke or John, any one of the Gospels that document his life, personality, and purpose. We can see Jesus. No longer is the hand empty. We can make a choice because we see the personality of Jesus and we know his purpose. The vagueness of "seeing God in everything," and thus in nothing, is replaced by the reality of knowing God in knowing Christ.

## Living with God in Two-way Prayer

One of the realities of God in our living with him is his desire that we reflect his image, much as a mirror reflects our images. What happens? Like a mirror that "decides" it no longer wishes to be round, but square, and cracks itself out of shape, we decide we no longer wish to live within the boundaries God intended. We crack and reflect a distortion of God. Neither the cracked mirror nor the cracked Christian can reflect the reality for which we were created. Unlike the inanimate mirror, however, we have power to heal our cracks and to change our distortion to a more accurate and shining reflection of our God. The healing process is done in conscious steps: Recognition, Rejection, and Reconstruction.

The distortion came because we wanted to reset our boundaries. The new boundaries included negative behavior, unlike the goodness and integrity of God whom we were meant to reflect.

When we *recognize* our negative behavior and come to terms with it by *rejecting* it as the way we want to live, Jesus will *reconstruct* us to wholeness again by showing us his love. "I demand that you love each other as much as I love you. And here is how to measure it—the greatest love is shown when a person lays down his life for his friends" (John 15:12 LB). But we must admit the negative behavior to God and forgive ourselves, knowing that God will forgive us also. "If we confess our sins, he is faithful and just to forgive us our sins and to cleanse us from all unrighteousness" (1 John 1:9). The word "confess" means "to agree with God concerning." And the word "sin" means "missing the mark." Thus we agree with God concerning the fact that there are areas in life where we have "missed the mark."

Through the Bible God has instructed us to live within a certain framework for our own mental, physical, and sociological well-being. When we step out of that framework on our own accord, we harm ourselves. It creates tremendous disharmony in body, mind, and spirit. We experience a vague or pronounced dissatisfaction in life. When we recognize that we have done this, we say, "Oh, that was a mistake. I shouldn't have done that. Lord, forgive me and help me not to make that mistake again."

In our living with God, we come to terms with unresolved, unconfessed negatives, one by one. Confessing these negatives to God is a tremendous catharsis, a cleansing of the subconscious memory bank. As we reject the negative thoughts, we can replace them with positive ones. That way the negative doesn't return as quickly. How can I think positive thoughts? The most powerful positive thoughts to replace negative ones are those that come from the Person, Jesus Christ. All of Jesus Christ's attributes, his total Person, can indwell us if we ask him to. We study him. If we fill our minds with thoughts of him, he will sweeten the bitterest memory. As we and Christ walk through life's experiences together, our friendship grows into a beautiful intimacy and we begin living with God. Just as Isaiah lovingly promises, "O my people . . . you shall weep no more. . . . He will answer you. Though he give you . . . adversity and . . . affliction, yet he will be with you to teach you—with your own eyes you will see your Teacher. And if you leave God's paths . . . you will hear a Voice behind you say, 'No, this is the way; walk here' " (Isa. 30:19–21 LB).

An experience that deepened Arvella Schuller's trust in Christ began one evening in her bedroom. She was hurrying through the routine of packing her husband's suitcase for an important trip to New York City. Her mind was in its usual state of sorting out a host of complex problems dealing with T.V. productions, building projects, mothering five children, and being the wife and confidante of Bob Schuller. Briefly she noticed a curious little mass of wires on the mantle in the bedroom. Quickly she put the last minute things in her husband's case and dismissed the "little wires" from her mind.

The next day her baby-sitter called and asked if Mrs. Schuller had found the dental retainers she had left on the fireplace mantle. Arvella checked, but the little wires were gone.

"Oh, Mrs. Schuller, it will cost me $125.00 to replace those retainers for my teeth!"

Arvella promised to look for them. She had never seen dental retainers before. Could she possibly have thought they were something her young daughter played with? Maybe they were in the toy drawer. In her haste could she have thought it was a useless mass of wires and have thrown them away? She searched everywhere—she emptied wastebaskets, ransacked drawers, checked the floor, and even looked in the trash compactor. Finally, she went into Two-way Prayer. The steps she took were these: *stop, look, love* and *listen.*

1) *Stop*—She stopped and quieted her physical body; she established mental silence.

2) *Look*—She looked *within* and examined her motive for wanting to find the retainers. She purified her thoughts—releasing fears and resentments.

3) *Love*—She sought the love of God and imagined Christ beside her.

4) *Listen*—She asked him where the retainers might be and waited for his answer.

The answer she received was that the retainers were in the trash compactor. Even though she had looked there before, she looked again. She didn't find them!

Throughout her hectic day she looked and prayed. If she had a few minutes, she quieted herself for Two-way Prayer and the answer came back, "In the trash compactor." She looked again. They weren't there! She prayed three or four more times. The answer was still the same.

Her concern for the teenager's retainers began to magnify. *I don't want her and her mother to think Christians are careless and irresponsible,* she thought. Just then Sheila, Arvella's beautiful-in-her-twenties daughter, came home.

"Honey," Arvella said in one last desperate attempt, "each time I've gone into Two-way Prayer I get the same answer. While I make supper, will you 'piece' through the trash compactor for the retainers?"

Sheila, with painstaking perserverance, piece after begrimed piece, finally reached the very bottom of the compactor. To her utter astonishment there unharmed, lay the delicate dental appliance. It was unbent and in perfect condition!

Arvella lives with God knowing he is working with her as a Friend to help her be a successul wife and mother.

*Finding Success and Prosperity in Two-way Prayer*

Success, however, is different from prosperity. Some people achieve success but never find prosperity. Others find prosperity without ever achieving success. The latter group is desperately unhappy. They have achieved material riches without finding and accomplishing that for which they were born. The billionaire, Howard Hughes, died an unhappy, unfulfilled man, rich but poor.

Another unhappy man I know was a patient in our office. He married the daughter of a multimillionaire. Her father owned four skyscrapers in New York City. The patient was chronically depressed and ulcer-prone. He said, "I am an independently wealthy man. I don't have to work. I can have anything I want, and I'm so miserable I don't know what to do." Two years later he visited our office again. With a genuine smile on his face and a bounce in his step, he said, "My divorce became final last month. I couldn't be happier or more broke!"

He shared his inner feelings of wanting to work to prove to himself what he could do. It used to be every time he got a job, the establishment found out who his father-in-law was and promoted him to the top. He knew his promotions weren't based on his own accomplishments. The trap of prestige, power, money, and in-laws was stifling his ingenuity and integrity. He wanted to experience success before prosperity.

Jesus Christ was probably the most successful person who ever lived. He accomplished that for which he was born. He died penniless, yet fulfilled. Though poor he was rich. "Who for the joy that was set before him endured the cross, despising the shame . . ." (Heb. 12:2), that many might find in him eternal life. At his birth the angel said, "Thou shalt call his name Jesus for he shall save his people from their sins" (Matt. 1:21). One of the seven last words he spoke was, "Father, forgive them" (Luke 23:24). Born to teach us, love us, and show us the Father, he did it. He lived and died for us!

D. L. Moody, the great preacher from England, died with only a few material possessions. On his deathbed he said, "If this is dying, it's wonderful. My room is flooded with angels." The hallmark of a successful man is joy and contentment at the end of his life.

A radiant Christian woman came up to me and said, "I'm rich! It's only money I don't have." She had found success without prosperity. Some people find both.

R. G. LeTourneau, designer of huge earthmoving equipment, was a successful *and* a prosperous man. He was a fine Christian like J. C. Penney who was also successful and prosperous. Colonel Sanders, who established the Kentucky Fried Chicken chain, experienced success and prosperity.

The Bible has much to say about the laws of prosperity. God prospered Abraham, David, and Solomon. If we need prosperity to make us happy, God will help us find a way to be prosperous.

## Eight Principles of Success from Business

The laws of success and prosperity have been studied by top business concerns in our country. Many fine motivational programs have been established. Businesses find these programs effective in increasing sales and profits. Now, motivational lecturers and experts from the field of the behavioral sciences give us eight basic principles for successful living which they have observed in the lives of hundreds of top leaders in our country. They are as follows:

"1) Your attitude should be successful, but not arrogant of mind.

2) Deal with your problems—don't bury them.

3) Be mentally strong and well-disciplined.

4) Believe in your inner self—it is powerful.

5) Be kind, honest, fair, but firm.

6) Keep your thoughts and drives pure.

7) Be known as a man of your word—where there is misunderstanding, bring understanding—be a peacemaker.

8) Be dedicated—don't give up." [1]

From my experience in watching the businessman get excited about prayer I have learned how God blesses the man who lives within the framework of the law of success. What top executive wouldn't love to have a company filled with workers who followed these principles! No wonder large corporations pay up to $500.00 for an employee to take a weeklong seminar to hear these eight concepts for success. The company prospers, the executive prospers, and the workers prosper.

*Eight Principles of Success from God*

Those very principles that are fostering success in the business world will bring success in your Two-way Prayer experience. The principles are not new. Jesus the Nazarene taught them two thousand years ago. The eight guidelines exactly parallel the eight Beatitudes. Too often we have casually read the distilled wisdom of the Sermon on the Mount without trying to make it a way of life.

Truth is truth. Truth will always bear itself out in time. No matter who says it, if it is true, it is eternal. Imagine all the books of truth and wisdom written through the ages being gathered into one massive library. If all the wise Western and Eastern philosophers, ancient and modern, and in-between, could be summed up and condensed into one volume, that one volume would have to be the Bible. If all the wisdom in the Bible could be condensed into one sermon, that sermon would have to be the Sermon on the Mount. If the Sermon on the Mount could be lived without flaw in one person's life, that life would have to be the life of Jesus Christ. If the innermost secret of his love and power were put into just eight simple principles, those principles would have to be the Beatitudes.

They are the summation of Jesus' personality. He lived and proved every one. The more Christlike we become, the closer our personalities will parallel the Beatitudes, and the more balanced and normal our minds will be. The opposite is also true. The headlines in the *Los Angeles Times* read, "The further a person gets from God, the more neurotic he becomes." A healthy and robust inner soul understands and thrives on the Beatitudes.

I recognize that the Beatitudes are far beyond us in terminology. For years I felt no one could ever live by these truths today. Yet, I didn't feel they were given by Christ only for some future use. This is the way Christ wants his children to be. He certainly was all of these things.

Why, then, did I feel so uncomfortable thinking of someone saying to me, "You're a meek person"? That thought sent goose bumps up my spine! I had an archaic interpretation of those words and phrases. My own locked-in definition was keeping me from indulging in the mighty truth that has now brought success and joy into living as never before.

It seems we've put a nineteenth century wall of traditionalism around Matthew 5:3–12 so that we've been afraid of fresh, new meanings. We've had the Beatitudes as long as we've had John 3:16. Yet people can become emotionally involved with John 3:16 while the Beatitudes fall on deaf ears. Our problem has been that we've interpreted these powerful principles with singular vision—theologically only. In the Bible we are taught to be "doers of the Word" (James 1:22). To do that, we need to understand the Bible experientially as well as theologically. In other words, we need to get emotionally involved with the Beatitudes. We need to feel them, taste them, smell them, see them, and hear them! From a psychological and theological interpretation we discover a breakthrough in meaning that is practical.

The closer we live within the framework of the Beatitudes, the more like Christ we become, the greater our fellowship with him, and the more successful we'll be in the enjoyment and workings of Two-way Prayer.

Just the opposite is true, too. When we violate one of the Beatitudes, we begin to step out of God's framework. We begin to lose our mental and spiritual balance. Conflicts, confusions, and apathy set in and we lose the serenity and peace of mind that come through Two-way Prayer.

I can't stress strongly enough how important it is to check ourselves often with the guidelines of the eight Beatitudes, if we want to be successful in Two-way Prayer. In the next several chapters let's consider how and why the Beatitudes are related to Two-way Prayer.

# 6

# *Turbulent Waters*

*"Blessed are the poor in spirit . . ."*

The Jerusalem Bible translates this as "Happy are the poor in spirit." Some translations say, "Blessed are the humble." We know Jesus is not talking about being financially poor but rather about having a specific mental attitude. What do our minds need to lack to be humble? We need an absence of egotistical pride. A minister told me a careful word study going back to the original language would translate this more accurately: "successful but not arrogant." That idea we can understand. This the businessman understands. This we can do!

## Successful But Not Arrogant

What are the natural rewards for being nonarrogant? ". . . for theirs is the kingdom of heaven." The Jews knew the meaning of the word kingdom. They had kings. The kingdom was a place where all of their needs were met, a place of power and authority. The word heaven can be translated "within" or "the abode of God." We are told we are the temples of God. We know he dwells within us. A fresh translation of the first Beatitude could be, "Happy are the successful but not arrogant, for theirs is the power within."

Arrogance is an enemy to Two-way Prayer. It can clothe itself in many costumes. Arrogance sets up housekeeping in the second level of the mind, the conscious. We need to beware of this when we have had a loving and personal dialogue with Christ. As we go from the God-conscious level and pass through all the levels of the mind and out into the sensory world, we have taken

72

that exquisite experience through the level of the conscious mind. Arrogance may whisper, ever so piously, "This is fantastic! I can't understand why my wife doesn't want to spend more time in Two-way Prayer!" That thought is subtly wrapped in well-meaning self-righteousness. Take that thought back into the inner closet and ask God, "Why doesn't my wife spend more time in Two-way Prayer?" What do you think God's answer would be? My experience with similar questions has been answers something like this:

1) "She is not ready for Two-way Prayer. She has other lessons to learn first."
2) "I will deal with her in my own way. Let me be God."
3) "Never mind. You have more than you can handle just maintaining your own spiritual life."

Arrogance can manifest itself in phrases like, "God told me . . ." while talking with others. Communicating with God has been fairly rare in our generation. People don't understand, "God told me. . . ." They become awed, scared or disgusted. Out of love and sensitivity for others such statements are a "no-no." We must be careful not to meddle in other people's lives. It is better for each person to learn to balance his own mind, body, and spirit with God, rather than to depend on others to be a mediator. The Bible says, "There is . . . one mediator between God and men, the man Christ Jesus" (1 Tim. 2:5).

Ego, man's pride, is too vulnerable at this point. If God tells us things about other people, it is usually to help us better understand them. Success in Two-way Prayer as well as in one's secular life can be won without arrogance as long as we remember our success has come from God, not from self.

When the dentist, Frank Hutchinson, asked me to go into Two-way Prayer regarding his patient, I knew the dangers of such a request. They were:

• The possibility of the conscious mind getting involved when an answer to a question is forced. The stress of trying to make something happen makes our minds tense! Our answer then could come from some other level than the God-level.
• If the conscious mind did get involved, it could be harmful to the patient, since it would be man's answer.

- If the answer from God were true, others would come with their requests. Soon I would become a mini-god.
- If people used me as a crutch, they would never be motivated to experience God first-hand.

It was kind of God to warn me but merciful of him still to give me the urgent answer.

## Our Positive Minds and Two-way Prayer

Jesus also tried to help us understand that true Christianity is measured by the thoughts and intents of the mind, not only in pious behavior. The sensitivity and beauty of prayer is easily tarnished by selfish, proud, negative or fearful thinking. It seems strange how many people still measure a person's Christianity by what he does rather than by what he is.

If a person is living in beautiful fellowship with God, prayer will be an active living reality. The effectiveness of one's prayer is not determined by his doctrinal beliefs, nor by how correct his theology is, nor by his precise keeping of the Ten Commandments. I have known Catholics, Jews, and Protestants who have walked intimately close, moment by moment, with Christ. I have known people who were involved in adultery, drugs, or alcoholism—and God was speaking gently to them in prayer, helping them overcome a weakness with which they were wrestling. They struggled, moaned, repented, and God stood there with his arms wide open. They saw him. They told me so. I have talked with biblically saturated people who were so sure they had all the right answers about what God wanted and didn't want for others. Interestingly enough, for some reason many of these people say Two-way Prayer doesn't work for them. I wonder—could it be they missed the meaning of the first Beatitude? I wonder if they miss the "be" attitude entirely?

## Growing from Pain

Following the second Beatitude is also essential in Two-way Prayer:
"Blessed are they that mourn: for they shall be comforted."

Mourning means to feel sorrow. A strong emotion that tells us our inner selves are seriously hurt, sorrow causes us to rally the forces of healing to the soul.

What are some of the things we mourn over? We mourn the loss of a loved one, or the death of a goal we have had. We can also feel sorrow when a plan goes awry or a dream is broken. Deep disappointments and discouragements can cause sorrow. We may feel sorrow for some wrong in our lives. The wrong may be destroying a virtue that could grow in our personality. We find some people who are chronic mourners over a memory or bad childhood experience.

The Beatitude says "blessed" are they for "they shall be comforted." The word "blessed" gives us the impression something is to be gained from mourning. In our pain we learn new knowledge and sensitivity. Great insights and special wisdom come through deep trials. As we are forced to think and care for our inner feelings we learn much about ourselves. God reveals deep and precious truths when he gives his comfort. We learn his ability to heal where no one else can reach.

Sometimes the hurt is too deep even to recognize; yet it festers like an infection and spreads to other facets of our personality.

One of my students in Michigan was a beautiful brown-eyed, blond mother. She gallantly carried a wide grin and cheerful personality. For weeks she covered up her nervous and fearful struggles. One day she came to me and said, "Why is Satan after me when I pray?"

I asked her to explain.

"I've had such fearful dreams and visual experiences lately."

Laura [1] was a lucid pictorial thinker. She saw images clearly and in vivid colors. Her dreams and visual pictures were similar. Most of them had to do with fearful sexual activities, usually with women. I said, "Laura, those images are not from Satan. You are a Christian and Satan cannot enter the holy temple where God is alive and well! God speaks in images. I believe he is trying to tell you there is a fear coming between you and him. You need to deal with that fear. It's hampering your Christian growth. Laura, what are you mostly afraid of?"

She burst into tears. "May I make an appointment to see you sometime?" A few days later Laura came to my office. She sat down and sighed. With poise and confidence she began to speak:

"I don't know what's the matter. I'm so depressed and afraid. All my church friends say it's Satan. They tell me he's out to get me because I'm trying this Two-way Prayer thing."

I asked her how she felt about it.

"I don't know. Something tells me to continue but, Perky, I'm afraid. I dream of women seducing me. I make love to them . . . why? I'm so afraid! A good Christian friend of mine left her husband last year for another woman! We went around with that couple. I think of her all the time. I don't want that to happen to me!"

"You mean you have fears of getting involved with another woman?" I asked.

"Oh, no! I can't stand to have a woman touch me. We have this really sweet elderly lady in our church who is always mothering me. I like her a lot but I'm afraid of her. When she pats me on the arm, I go home and feel it all day long. She asks our family over for dinner with their family and things like that. I'm afraid to get too close to her. What's wrong with me?"

"Laura, tell me about your own mother," I urged. She lowered her eyes. Her face became sullen.

"When I was nine years old my father came home drunk. I was in the room with my mother. My father walked in the door, took out a gun, and shot her in cold blood. I saw it all."

"Oh, Laura, how terrible! . . . How do you feel toward your father now?"

"I've forgiven him. He went to prison. I feel sorry for him, too. He suffered a great deal. I have no resentment toward him."

"How old was your mother?"

"She was just thirty-five. Perky, she was so beautiful."

"Laura, I believe she was since you're her daughter."

Laura swallowed hard. She couldn't talk. I handed her a box of tissues. As she covered her face with both hands, her shoulders and chest began to heave. I knew the body language. It said that down deep in her soul was great "mourning" for something she needed to face. A tranquilizer would never heal this kind of pain, nor codeine, nor alcohol. She was a lovely committed Christian. Why should she hurt so? Can a husband heal this kind of hurt? A close friend? Who can heal these imbedded lacerations of the mind?

Laura wanted to talk but it was difficult. Gently I told her to take her time. For forty-five minutes she struggled between words and phrases to put a sentence together.

## God's Healing Comfort

"Oh, God," I prayed, "put Your big strong arms around her and pour Your strength into her so she can put it all together. Help me to know what to say. Don't let me say too much . . . and don't let me say too little!"

"Perky, I haven't thought of these things for years. I've never told anyone, but I must tell you!

"After my mother died, my father went to prison. I went to live with my aunt. One night while I was sleeping my uncle came home drunk. He crawled into bed with me . . . he began to fondle me. I was terrified. I didn't dare to resist him, but I didn't know what to do. The next morning I wanted to tell someone. I was confused and afraid but I never told a soul. Then, I remember about a year later I was swimming. An older teenage boy ran and dove off the diving board. When he came up, he came near me and grabbed me between the legs. Again I was afraid but I didn't dare tell my aunt. We weren't very close. . . ."

"Laura, are you afraid you might be a lesbian?" I asked.

"I don't know. Can a Christian become a lesbian? Why do I have such thoughts toward women? Is it Satan? I've rebuked him and rebuked him. I have this book on *Dealing with the Devil and How to Resist the* . . . ."

"No-no-no-no, Laura! Satan is real but this is God!! He's trying to help you resolve this fear once and for all! He can prove his power to heal and bring wholeness to a shattered memory. No one else can do that as well as God! Laura, young girls in their preteens need their mothers. Through no fault of your own, you lost yours. You had some fearful experiences indelibly pressed into your subconscious mind with a strong emotion. You needed to talk to your mother about your fears. She wasn't there. You needed her. Have you been reaching out to her ever since? Could it be every woman you see represents the mother you needed? Do you feel pulled toward her and become afraid of this strong attraction?"

She nodded "yes."

I suggested we go into a Two-way Prayer experience, explaining what we would do in detail. She agreed. I told her to open herself up to God as she had to me. I made it clear that I was no psychiatrist, nor did I pretend to be, but that Jesus was the Great Psychiatrist, and in prayer he could heal her psyche. I prepared her by saying we would use imagination and imagery, but we would not *try* to make anything happen. We would let the Holy Spirit do his mighty healing. When Laura was comfortable, she closed her eyes, becoming relaxed and mentally still. I gave her time to get rid of any negative emotions other than the fear we were dealing with.

Finally I said, "Now, follow me closely. See yourself sitting here in a chair in my office. Imagine Jesus opening the door and coming into the room. Stand up and take his hand. Outside the door is a pink cloud. You and Jesus will leave and he will hold you tightly. As you leave, see yourself and Jesus getting on the cloud. The cloud gently rises. You feel safe and secure and happy. The cloud is going higher and higher. It is traveling over the city and to a time, many years ago, when in your childhood, you and your mother were especially close. The cloud is lowering, and you and Jesus step off. When you 'see' your mother tell her all the things you've wanted to tell her as a child. Imagine what she would have said back to you." I paused for about ten minutes. There were many tears but I knew the Holy Spirit was speaking. I didn't want to interrupt those sacred moments.

I prayed, "God, give me the thoughts, the sensitivity, and the discernment to help Laura. If nothing else, help her to feel my love, my empathy, my understanding. She is so ashamed to admit these things!"

I spoke to Laura and said, "Tell your mother you and Jesus have to go now. See yourself get back on the cloud, travel back in time to now, January, and get off the cloud. Say, 'Thank You' to Jesus and sit in the chair in my office. For the next few moments think 'God, Immanuel, Messiah' on each breath. Spend a short time now thinking about God's love for you. If you have any questions about the exercise, ask him."

I waited another five minutes. She was still in prayer.

The tears stopped.

Her face began to clear. The redness receded. An almost heavenly expression came over her serene face. The corners of her mouth curled in a smile. I said, "Tell God you have to go now, and on the next three breaths say, 'Thank You, Father.' "

She sat pensively, eyes staring down into her lap. There was a prevailing peacefulness emanating from her. I waited . . . and waited. After five more minutes she looked up at me and said, "Wow, that was tremendous!"

We spent the next half hour talking about her experience. God led her to discuss feelings with Christ she had denied to herself—such as the fear she had that her husband didn't really love her. All her questions were answered with gentle and pure wisdom. She knew her new understanding was from above. "Blessed are they that mourn: for they shall be comforted."

*Comfort and Productivity*

Laura came to my office six months later. She said, "Perky, I want you to know that not even the slightest fear of women has ever crossed my mind since that Two-way Prayer experience last January. It's been wonderful. I'm totally healed of every one of those fears. Besides that . . . I'm writing Sunday school material for preteen-age girls now. I've always wanted to, but before that prayer experience, I could not bring myself to the preteen level. Now it just flows. Isn't God great!"

He surely is! I have a feeling she couldn't write a Sunday school lesson for preteen-age girls until her own painful memories of those years were healed. Now she is creative and productive for God.

It seems as though the anguish of these incidents was programmed into Laura's subconscious mind. Night and day she had them, on a subliminal or subconscious level. She was not consciously aware of the memory, but the strong emotions drastically affected her personality. Afraid to touch women, she felt guilty and unworthy of her husband's love. Where these feelings came from she didn't know. Her only explanation was that Satan was harassing her. Isn't it beautiful that we can allow ourselves to go into our memory computer, hand-in-hand with Christ? We can let him sort it all out for us, give us the answers to comfort and quiet the troubled waters of the soul, and the harassment of past memories. Laura became emotionally and experientially involved with the second Beatitude. Jesus stilled the stormy breakers in the Sea of Galilee and he can quiet the troubled waters of the mind!

Sometime later, my husband and I were having dinner with a psychologist friend. I told her about the experience with Laura.

I asked, "In your psychological practice have you ever seen or heard of a case where such a fear of lesbianism was healed as thoroughly and quickly?"

She thought for a moment or two and said, "No . . . never!" She was amazed and delighted at the healing power of Two-way Prayer.

Imagery and visualization is the nonlanguage of the subconscious mind. When Christ is in that imagery, it becomes a prayer. In Two-way Prayer we must become aware of our negative emotions. They stunt both personality and spiritual growth. Therefore, the second enemy of Two-way Prayer is negative emotion!

*Our Reflection and Our World*

When we sow negative thoughts, we certainly reap negative behavior. Negative thoughts are physically destructive to brain tissue. They set up toxic chemicals that act like poison to the cells. Negative thoughts age one's appearance as well. They increase the wrinkles and deepen the facial lines. We pay dearly for our negatives. They invade the subconscious mind and reflect themselves on our personality twenty-four hours a day. Negative thoughts haunt and hurt us until we resolve them.

After we understand a little about how the mind works, we can learn why it is essential to be a positive thinker. Psychology, business, and medicine agree that it is helpful to be a positive thinker. But Jesus made it a command, "Whatsoever things are pure, whatsoever things are lovely, whatsoever things are of good report—think on these things" (Phil. 4:8). James tried to tell us to be positive and creative even when adverse trials come our way.

> Dear brothers, is your life full
> of difficulties and temptations?
> Then be *happy* for when the way is
> rough, your patience has a chance
> to grow. So let it grow, and don't
> try to squirm out of your problems.
> For when your patience is finally
> in full bloom, then you will be
> ready for anything, strong in
> character, full and complete
> (James 1:2–4 LB).

James was a true possibility thinker!

# 7

# *Avenue to God's Thoughts*

The mind is a mansion. It has many rooms and God lives there! He has giant treasures for us—treasures of joy and contentment, wisdom and success. We can have them. They're ours. They are our birthright. Jesus said, "I am come that they might have life and have it more abundantly" (John 10:10). He has given us the entire world! We're rich!

## A Room Full of Gold

It's as though he had a room full of gold and said, "It's all yours, I want you to have it . . . when you can handle it. If I let you have it before you can handle it, it would destroy you! I am a God of abundance. Look at my universe. See my lavish generosity in creation. I would give you wealth if:

- It wouldn't consume all of your attention so that you forget me.
- You wouldn't flaunt it before a fellow man who wasn't ready for his 'room of gold.' This would make him jealous and cause him to feel his weakness all the more.
- You wouldn't become arrogant of mind.
- You wouldn't become self-centered, forgetting to heal the wounds of your neighbor.
- You would keep all your motives pure as you spent the gold.
- You would not lust after the power that would become yours. More important than earthly riches is your priceless soul. For some people I need to take away earthly goods, that their soul may prosper. Some people can prosper both ways."

*Well-Disciplined and Responsive*

How do we prepare ourselves to prosper both ways? The key is in the third Beatitude:

"Blessed are the meek: for they shall inherit the earth."

When Jesus spoke these words to the Jews in that day, they knew what "meek" meant. The Jews had horses and knew how valuable a "meeked" horse was. They also knew it took hours, weeks, and years of training to make a horse meek. Some horses were too stubborn and self-willed, in spite of countless hours of training, ever to learn "meekness."

We can watch a horse trainer; as onlookers we can view the work-out exercises. The rider and horse move together in the corral, around the track, over the hurdles. It's beautiful to watch a well-trained horse. Perhaps we watch several horses, then finally the trainer takes out his prize horse. He's been training it for a horse show. With pride and confidence he rides around the ring. Suddenly the horse goes into a gallop, then a canter . . . slows and stops. He poses as he would in a horse show. After ten minutes, he straightens his position and turns a complete circle slowly to the right . . . stops . . . and turns a complete circle to the left. He lifts his head high and struts parade-style over to us. The astonishing thing about this demonstration is that not once did we see the trainer give the horse a signal. We didn't hear any commands given to the horse. We ask the trainer, "How did the horse know what to do?"

The trainer explains, "This is a *meeked* horse. He is favored above all my horses because he is strong and well-disciplined. I give him signals but no one sees them. I press my right ankle in, ever so gently, and he turns right. I press my left ankle in, and he turns left. If I shift my weight on the saddle, that is another signal. If the judges see my signals, I lose points."

To the Jew the word "meek" meant "well-disciplined." It denotes strong character. It is not a "milk-toast," mousy word. "Well-disciplined" makes sense. If we are well-disciplined, Jesus said we will inherit the earth. The word takes on a new dimension when, as some Bible translators do, we add the thought of gentleness. A gentle, well-disciplined child is one in whom the parents delight. Such a child doesn't need the harsh punishment that a self-willed child needs. A parent simply whispers a suggestion and the child obeys. When God whispers suggestions to us, we're wise to obey promptly. Obedience would save us time and heartaches.

In Two-way Prayer God gives us inspiration. If we act on those thoughts, he gives another. An entire lovely plan is unfolded, step by step, lesson by lesson. If we procrastinate, he will wait until we've learned the first lesson before going on to the next. If we procrastinate too long, he gently nudges us along. If our procrastination turns into rejection of the idea altogether, we lose a tremendous treasure or receive a harsh correction.

## Overcoming Procrastination

This happened to me last summer. I had spent six months traveling, giving seminars, handling speaking engagements, and counseling. My schedule had become so rigid, the family was beginning to suffer. (I thought so, but they didn't!) Certainly, my housework needed my attention. All at once several things were canceled and I had a glorious ten days open in June.

When I went into Two-way Prayer, I asked, "God, why the opening? I love it, but I'm sure You have a reason for it. What do You want me to do in those ten days?"

The answer came, "Do your spring housecleaning."

"Oh sure," I said, "that will be fun!" I really love a sparkling clean house but mine had gotten a little dim around the edges. I had great intentions!

The next few days I started to clean. I found that as I stayed home, I was on the phone more. Friends, whom I had been neglecting, began to call. Because neglect is contrary to the law of friendship, I found myself saying, "Yes" to luncheons and fun things. My house didn't get cleaned—all that summer!

Early in July, I lost a watch that a treasured friend had given me at Easter. I looked everywhere. My close friends began asking,

"Why don't you go into Two-way Prayer and ask God where it is?" It was hard to explain. When I went into Two-way Prayer, I really didn't *want* to ask God where it was. It didn't feel "right." I would have "forced" the question. I became more embarrassed as the weeks went along. The people in our congregation asked, "Did you ask God in Two-way Prayer where your watch is?" Every time I led a meeting and every time I spoke I needed a "timekeeper" because I didn't have a watch. Finally I made myself ask God in Two-way Prayer if he wanted to tell me where my watch was. The answer came, "I have a very important lesson in this for you." I felt sort of excited, for I love to learn new things.

In August, we traveled to Michigan with our family. My husband, who is usually my "timekeeper" in the early morning hours, was tired of having to roll over, look at his watch, and say, "5:30." One day he said, "Let's get you a watch! This is ridiculous." And so he bought me one.

After a marvelous vacation, we returned to California in mid-September to a happy, bouncing, eager-to-get-started-in-fall activities church family. Our children were bustling off to college and high school, but I was still faced with the same grimy house. There was no way I could, in all good conscience, leave my house until it was deep, deep cleaned. It was tremendously difficult, now, to plan meetings, entertain committees, get the children settled, and do my "spring cleaning." But I did it. I started in the family room and worked through the house to the bedrooms. The master bedroom was the last room to be cleaned.

As I was cleaning the bed with Lysol-water (all nurses have to wipe the mattresses with Lysol-water!), I flipped the mattress over. To my amazement, in the middle of the bed, tucked between mattress and spring, was my treasured watch. It must have slipped off my wrist the previous July as I tucked the sheets in. The words, "I have a very important lesson in this for you," came back to me.

I thought of the third Beatitude, "Blessed are the gentle and well-disciplined: for they shall inherit the earth." If I had deep-cleaned the house even in July, I would have found my watch.

If I had not procrastinated, I could have saved my husband a hundred dollars. That watch waited there until I obeyed God's suggestion.

I lost spiritual progress, too. All summer I became concerned that I hadn't received any new creative thoughts during the Two-way Prayer experiences. God waited until I acted on the last instruction he gave. After I cleaned the house and found my watch, all kinds of innovative ideas came to me in prayer.

I certainly became experientially involved in this third Beatitude. Indeed, I'm still trying to learn to be meek, but at least when my living prayers become dead, I can usually pinpoint my problem. For me, this Beatitude is the one I usually violate. It is extremely sensitive to self-willfulness. Self-will and procrastination are two more enemies of Two-way Prayer.

Self-will and procrastination are enemies to success in marriage. They are also enemies to success in business. A well-disciplined worker is usually the one who gets the promotion over the worker with even greater ability who isn't disciplined. Happy, indeed, are the meek.

## Self-worth and a Quest

Business motivators list another guideline to "fame and fortune." They say, "Believe in your inner self—it is powerful."

Blessed are they which do hunger and thirst after righteousness:
for they shall be filled.

The inner self truly is powerful. From the inner self comes ideas that move the world. To believe in ourselves, we need to like ourselves. Some people don't feel they are worth much.

Just how much is an individual worth? In today's inflationary market our body is worth only a few dollars in terms of its chemical content. How much are we worth to the person in our world who loves us the most? Is that person a mother? A wife? A husband? If someone wanted us and were in a position to "buy" us from our loved one, how much money would it take for them to say, "It's a deal!"?

How much, then, do we think we're worth to God? The price God pays measures our true worth. If someone were bargaining with God for our soul, how much money would God give in exchange for us? The Bible tells us, "For a soul is far too precious to be ransomed by mere earthly wealth. There is not enough of it in all the earth to buy eternal life for just one soul, to keep it out of hell" (Ps. 49:8, 9 LB). Not enough gold in all the earth to buy us? We're worth an incredible amount to God!

What was he willing to give for us? God gave his Son Jesus Christ who died on the cross. God did this to restore us to a close relationship with himself. God was willing to give Jesus' life . . . to gain ours! Does that tell us what we're worth to God? We are worth as much to God as Jesus is worth to God! What an awesome thought: *I am worth Jesus Christ, to God.* Think it again, "I am worth Jesus Christ, to God." Say it aloud, "I am worth Jesus Christ, to God!"

*Overcoming Inferiority*

If we know we are worth that much to the God of our mammoth universe, why care what people *think* we're worth? Our worth is tremendous! The difficulty most of us have is that we lose sight of our true worth. We compare ourselves with other people. We see them excelling in areas in which we consider ourselves inferior. Feelings of inferiority may stem from our own interpretation of life. All of life is an interpretation of the mind. We may think we're not as good-looking as someone else, or as talented, or as wealthy. We may feel we have nothing to offer the world. Every day we meet people with charming personalities who have no particular accomplishment to offer but themselves. These people applaud the speaker, the soloist, the top executive, the TV star—yet they don't feel any less important. They have found a way to enjoy other peoples' inner treasures while they enjoy themselves as well.

I remember talking to my sister, Eunice, one afternoon. Joyce Landorf had just dropped in and I introduced her to Eunice. We chatted awhile. When Joyce left, I told Eunice the exciting things Joyce was doing. She was on her way to the studio to "cut" a record album, then to the TV studio for an interview, then to the radio station to record a week of fifteen-minute daily broadcast programs for women. I said, "Wouldn't it be wonderful to be beautiful and talented like Joyce?"

Eunice replied, "Oh, I don't know." I thought I detected a "sour grapes" attitude. I prodded, "What do you mean, 'I don't know'?"

"I'm glad for Joyce that she's beautiful and talented, but I have other things." Eunice wasn't being haughty—just humbly assertive. I laughed at my kid sister and said, "Such as. . . ."

"Such as—people say I'm a good listener," she smiled.

"Eunice, you're absolutely right. You have to be the best listener in the whole world!" And she is! She listens with her mind, not just her ears. Many, many times she has sorted out what I was trying to say, capsulated it into three or four words, and given it back to me in the form of a tactful question. "Gentle wisdom," that's my sister! She's no Joyce Landorf. Although she dearly loves Joyce, she loves herself, too.

We're worth everything to God. His heart would break if he lost us!

George W. Campbell was born blind with cataracts in both eyes. He didn't know he was blind until he was six years old. One day he was outdoors playing ball with neighborhood friends. A friend called to him and said, "Watch out, George, the ball is going to hit you!" Split seconds later, the ball hit him in the head. George went home crying. While his mother was putting a cold cloth on his head, George asked, "How did those boys know the ball was going to hit me?"

For the first time in George's life, his mother had to explain his blindness. "You see, George, most people have five senses like you have five fingers." She held his one little finger. "They have hearing." Then she took the ring finger: "They have taste." The third finger: "They have smell." The second finger: "They have touch." Then she held his thumb: "They have sight. Now, you have only four senses instead of five."

She picked up a ball and told George to put out four fingers instead of five. With his thumbs tucked in, he listened as she told him, "I'm going to throw this ball to you, and I want you to catch it."

George held out his hands. She threw the ball. George caught it.

"There, you see, George. You can do it! You can reach out and catch all the fun and opportunities in life with four senses instead of five."

And so George did. He went to school and learned and achieved. When he was eighteen years old, his physician came to him.

"George," he said, "there is a new surgical procedure for cataracts. We may be able to operate and give you your sight. I must tell you, also, the great risk we face. If we operate, you may not get your sight. In fact, it may ruin your chances of ever seeing again. Are you willing to take the risk?"

George nodded, "Yes."

In time, George had the operation. His eyes were bandaged during the healing process. Several days passed. The pressure of not knowing whether the operation was a success grew for George, the doctor, the nurses, and his mother. The day came for the doctor to remove the bandages. His mother was in the room. When the eye pads came off, George opened his eyes but couldn't see a thing. "I can't . . . I can't see," he said.

His anxious mother rushed closer to him and said, "George! George! Can you see me?"

George blinked his eyes. A fuzzy mass before him started to come into focus. His eyesight cleared. The first object George Campbell saw in life was the face of a sixty-two-year-old woman, wrinkled from years of toiling to teach and train him to "catch all of life." He looked down at the knotted and gnarled hands that had done washings and ironings to provide him the things he needed.

He said, "I opened my eyes and saw the beautiful face of my mother as if it were the face of an angel." The years of teaching, loving, and patient affection made her beautiful to him.

Later in life after George had seen many lovely women, he

still said, "She remained to me the most beautiful woman I'd ever seen. What we see is always an interpretation of the mind."

There are other physical weaknesses and disorders of the eyes besides cataracts. In fact, the most common physical weakness of the eyes results in either nearsightedness or farsightedness.

The major distortion of the mind's eye, however, is to grope in a maze of false concepts—probably the most common one being our lack of self-worth. We lose our perspective in the masses of people.

I often drive the expansive freeways in downtown Los Angeles. As I approach "the stack"—five freeways bridging on top of each other at one time—I'm enthralled at the engineering genius represented. Bumper to bumper in every direction are cars full of people. Thousands of them. At night, the lights form silver and red ribbons. The silver ribbon is created from a line of cars, four or five lanes broad for miles in one direction. Their white headlights fill in every available space. The red ribbon is formed by cars going in the opposite direction, showing only their red taillights. It's a glorious sight. Nevertheless, one can easily lose his feeling of importance in such a mass of humanity. Yet, each person in each car is a champion.

We are all champions—we're winners in God's sight. He knows it. Do we? We are not worthless. We never have been. Even without God we are not worthless. Without God we are *helpless* but not *worthless.* There certainly is a power in the inner self. That power is God. Some people find God by wanting him more than anything else. They hunger and thirst for him—they crave him. They read everything they can to learn more about him, and they go to lectures, seminars, church services. They talk to others. Daily they grow in their concept of God. It's more than a hobby to them. It's a driving life force.

### Finding God, Finding Wealth

Then there are others who find the power of God in the face of great difficulty or a devastating crisis. One such man was R. G. LeTourneau. A subcontractor on the Hoover Dam in Nevada, he lost all his money trying to complete the job. It seems he ran into a particular layer of rock that cost huge sums to drill through. LeTourneau hadn't planned on such expense, and he lost a fortune fulfilling his contract.

Exhausted and discouraged, Mr. LeTourneau turned to prayer, an internal activity. As he prayed, he began to thank God for what he had left. He had a strong body, a skillful pair of hands, and a brain that could think. "In my hour of greatest distress," said LeTourneau, "I found my greatest asset in the discovery of a Senior Partner. Everything I have—every worthwhile thing I have done—I owe to him."

R. G. LeTourneau had reached his lowest ebb externally. However, when he reconstructed his inner world through prayer, he released the power that changed his life.

LeTourneau was in partnership with God. He built heavy earth-moving equipment and became a millionaire. It is said of him that he gave 90 percent of his income, even before he became wealthy, to God's purposes. He kept 10 percent to live on. God gave this successful but not arrogant man his "room full of gold." When he turned to the Spirit of God within, he found the power to achieve. Blessed are they which do hunger and thirst after righteousness, for they shall be filled.

## A Thirst for God

In ancient times a student who hungered and thirsted after righteousness stopped beside a lake and questioned his teacher.

"Tell me, sir, how can I get to know God?"

The teacher took him out into the lake and told him to put his head under the water. As he did, the teacher held the student's head under water with his hand. The student struggled and fought to come to the surface. Still the teacher held his head firmly. Finally, in desperation the man gave one last gallant attempt to surface and came up sputtering and gasping for air.

"What . . . are you trying to do? I almost drowned! I couldn't get my breath!"

The teacher said, "Tell me, what were you thinking about all the time I held your head in the water?"

"Only one thing, sir. All I could think of was 'I want air' . . . 'I need air' . . . 'I've got to have air or I'll die!' "

"That's how badly you have to want God—and then you will know him!" the wise teacher replied.

In modern times we find God when all we can think of is, "I want God . . . I've got to have God or I'll die. . . ." When the fourth Beatitude becomes a principle of life, the promises that accompany it are ours.

"Seek ye first the kingdom of God, and his righteousness, and all these things shall be added unto you" (Matt. 6:33). The world has yet to see the creative treasures that lie dormant in the mind. By finding God, we will find ourselves.

An earnest seeker for God came to the Two-way Prayer Seminar. He had an intense hunger for God. I knew this because he was married and had two children, worked full time, and went to school. He was also writing his thesis for a Master's Degree. Yet his drive to learn about God in a fresh, new way caused him to carve out time from this intense schedule to take a six-week, twelve-hour course. It was the fourth time he had gone through the Two-way Prayer exercises.

John was a vivid pictorial thinker. When I told the class to imagine themselves in some quiet, beautiful place, he thought of the beaches in Hawaii. He had taken a trip there and the memory was a pleasant one. In his mind's eye he saw the deep blue ocean rolling in on the white sandy beach. Then I said, "Look up and see someone in the distance coming toward you. As he gets closer, notice that it's Jesus. See him come to you and call you by name. Now, tell him the thing uppermost in your mind." I waited. After leading the class through the entire exercise I closed the session.

John came to me and said, "I've just had an incredible experience. When Jesus came to me, I said, 'Jesus, my thesis outline is due next Tuesday morning. I don't see how I'm ever going to get it done.'

"Jesus said, 'Don't worry about it.'

"But," I said, "I don't even know what I'm going to use for my outline. Then I saw Jesus in living color, just like the people

I see in my dreams, go over to the wet sand. He bent over and with his finger wrote out the entire outline for my thesis! I have to hurry home now. I want to write it down before I forget it."

John went home and wrote his thesis. Five months later my husband and I were having lunch with John and his wife. They told us John had received an A– on his thesis. "And all these things shall be added unto you."

Thirsting and longing for righteousness helps us to know God. To know God we need to know our inner selves. It takes diligence to know one's self and one's own worth. Apathy shrugs, "Why bother?" Indifference lulls us with the futility of our worth. We have to ignore apathy, obey the nudgings of God, and take the risks in action. If the action is an error, with earnestness we search our souls to detect our motives. Through the soul-searching, we learn what a pure motive is, and what God wants. The more we long, search, hunger, and thirst for God's righteousness, the more power we have in our inner selves.

Indifference and apathy destroy our sensitivity to God, our searching for God and trying his answers. They hinder the thirsting and longing for righteousness and God. Indifference and apathy are enemies of Two-way Prayer.

# 8

# The Power of Forgiveness

I felt as if I had been in the presence of God all afternoon. My mind was at peace but vibrantly expanded. I had that awesome inner glow one feels after attending a hallowed worship service.

There were no organs or pianos, no stained glass windows. My kneeling bench was the tundra area in the Rocky Mountains of Estes Park, Colorado, where the tiny flowers carpeted the towering mountain cathedral. Mentally and spiritually, I knelt before God. He had created these tenacious plants with their delicate beauty which can withstand the 100-mile-an-hour winds on top of a 10,000-foot mountain. In spite of the skimpy topsoil, the flowers survive bitter cold, high winds, intense heat, and long periods of drought. No tree can grow in such an environment.

## The Tundra of the Soul

These little plants grow slowly and are easily crushed by the heel of man. Years ago the American Indian made the trails that wind through the ground cover across these mountains. The deliberate growth is so slow that in the past hundred years the flowers have not yet spread over the Indian paths. The heel of man is still evident.

It was July and large chunks of lingering winter snow were pocketed in the folds of huge rocks. The tough plants with their lavender, pink, yellow, blue, and white blossoms smiled next to the melting glaciers. There was a feeling of contentment and natural satisfaction in the clear, crisp air. I whispered a prayer, "It is Your world, God, and it is good!"

The "worship service" continued as we made our way down the mountain. God's mouthpiece for the excursion was Clare Albee, an earth science teacher at Loy Norrix High School in Kalamazoo, Michigan. This man probably lives as close to God as anyone I've met. That day he helped me see God the way he does. It was beautiful. Like an eloquent preacher, Mr. Albee shared his knowledge and love of creation in such a way that I felt breathlessly close to the Creator. In experiencing the balance of nature, I experienced a true re-creation within the mainspring of my soul.

In a few days we were totally refreshed and restored to God's unity of mind, spirit, and body. We were ready to return to our daily work world. It wasn't long before the serenity and peace of that vacation were punctured by the sharp edge of our civilization.

We drove into the parking lot of a fast-food restaurant. As our car engine stilled, halfway across the parking lot came a mother's shrill screech assaulting her six- or seven-year-old son.

"You stupid fool! Why didn't you lock the car as you came out? Do you want someone to steal it? When will you ever grow up and take responsibility? Now, hurry up and lock the door and get in here before someone else gets ahead of us!" The boy's shoulders slumped before the insensitivity of his mother's attack.

## "Extend the Vacation Feeling"

Already the heels of man were crushing the alpine flowers on the tundra of my soul. My vacation was starting to wear off. There is a way to preserve that feeling of wholeness one acquires by spending a few days close to nature. Centuries ago the heels of man crushed Jesus on the cross. Yet he told us his secret of how to extend the tranquil benefits of a vacation. In the fifth Beatitude he spoke to the people and said:

"Blessed are the merciful: for they shall obtain mercy."

Mercy is different from justice. Mercy is what we want from the hand of others when we have done wrong. Justice, or impartiality, is what we are willing to give others when they have done wrong. Mercy, or forgiveness, has a fraternal twin—grace or kindliness. Mercy and grace live side by side in the harmony of the Christlike personality. Mercy withholds that deserved punishment. Grace, on the other hand, gives a kindness to someone who has been rude to us, and bestows a blessing which hasn't been earned. Living daily with the mental attitude of being full of mercy and grace keeps our inner souls in balance.

The mother in the McDonald's parking lot could have shown kind behavior in training her child. Gently but firmly she could have said, "I want you to remember always to lock the car when we get out." Showing mercy would have been demonstrated by her willingness to pass over (without verbal punishment to her son's personality) her place in line in order to teach a life-lesson to her child. We can be kind, honest but firm when we are merciful.

## Space for Mercy and Grace

Mercy needs space in our personalities, however. To be full of mercy and compassion we cannot be filled with the negative emotions of vindictiveness and revenge. When we retaliate for wrongs others inflict upon us, or when we burden ourselves with grudges, these emotions act like poisons in our physical bodies. Much of our retaliation and vengeance have their roots in our own fears and resentments.

The slightest fear or resentment can now be detected by the delicate EEG. Many of us have carried fears and resentments for years without confessing them. They have become buried so deeply in our subconscious that we are unaware of them. Nevertheless, these culprits continue robbing us of health, happiness, and mercy. There are ways to discover if we are harboring the unwanted villains of vindictiveness, resentment, and fear.

## Find the Source of Fear

In Two-way Prayer, when one quiets his mind so that he is aware of certain subconscious thoughts, God can bring to his consciousness the fears and resentments that need to be confronted.

During the prayer exercise, I may give students time to contemplate their fears and resentments. The "computer" in the "memory bank" will open the "file" and take out a subliminal fear. We may become aware of it immediately, which is often the case with pictorial thinkers, or it may be several hours after our prayer session that the fear comes to mind. Whenever we think of it, it's time to get rid of it. I find power in the verse, "For God has not given us the spirit (or mind) of fear; but of power, and of love, and of a sound mind" (2 Tim. 1:7). When I realize the source of destructive fear, I can counteract it by drawing from God who overcomes fear with love and soundness of mind. God re-creates love and courage in us. That is inner strength.

I remember a lovely woman who came to me during a seminar. She asked, "Why, when I want to visualize Jesus, do I 'see' such weird things?"

As I began to inquire about her experiences, she explained, "When you said, 'See Jesus approaching,' all I saw was a series of eyes. Then I 'saw' a series of mouths. The eyes were hateful and skeptical, and the mouths were snarling, laughing, and mean."

I asked, "How did this make you feel?"

She said, "Afraid. Should I be afraid when I seek God in prayer?"

She wondered if Satan could be confusing her.

I said, "Mrs. Winters, I don't think it's Satan. What is the greatest fear you have about life at this time?"

Without a moment's hesitation, she replied, "I was just voted vice president of our church federation. I'll have to stand before people and talk. I've always been deathly afraid of speaking to an audience!"

When I asked her what she honestly thought the reaction of the people would be, she smiled sheepishly, "I think they will laugh and criticize me." She looked at me with enlightenment. "That was exactly what I saw in the eyes and mouths!"

I didn't have to say it, but to avoid any misunderstanding I asked, "Do you suppose that fear is coming between you and your intimate relationship with Christ?"

"Oh, yes! But how can I deal with it?"

I told her the answer lay in learning—

## SIX STEPS TO OVERCOMING FEAR

1) *Realize God's love for you.* "I have loved thee with an everlasting love; therefore with loving kindness have I drawn thee" (Jer. 31:3).

2) *Realize your worth to God.* Remember earlier I said, "God is willing to give his Son for you." This makes you worth Jesus Christ to God! Keep that in your mind. Repeat it over and over. If a negative thought like, *You are no good. What makes you think you can do a good job?* enters, think, *But I'm worth as much as Jesus. He loved me enough to die for me—that's everything for me. . . . Of course, I can do a good job. Jesus and God will be with me. They love me!*

3) *Do your work to please God.* When the fear of man comes to your mind—think of God. If you do a good job, man will pat you on the back. If your motives are not pure, even though the public praises you God will grieve. On the other hand, if you flounder and stutter, if man criticizes, yet your thoughts and intents are pure, God will pat you on the back. Work for God's praise. Man is too fickle.

4) *Be well prepared.* Do your homework well. Many times we have anxiety because we didn't do what we were supposed to do. For Mrs. Winter that meant practicing her speech in front of the mirror and then in front of her husband. If she could say it to her husband, it would be even easier to say it to ten thousand people!

5) *Keep a positive attitude.* When you walk on the platform:
   a) Think three things:
      (1) I am loved. (You are—by God!)
      (2) I am beautiful. (Inner beauty is 90 percent of the total impression.)
      (3) I have a secret. (This puts a glint in your eyes.

It makes people want to know what you have to share.)

Mrs. Winters needed to concentrate on these when she walked up to the platform.

    b) To overcome her fear of speaking, it was suggested she talk to one person at a time. Not to think of the sea of faces, but to see each woman as a person to love would help her to be less self-conscious.

6) *Remember 2 Timothy 1:7,* "For God hath not given us the spirit of fear. . . ."

I also instructed her to go into Two-way Prayer and give this fear to Christ. Then she could imagine him standing strong and confidently holding out his hand to her. Taking hold of his hand, she would walk with Christ up on the platform. His promise is, "I am with you, always . . ." (Matt. 28:20). He would stand at her side as she spoke. She could see herself speaking to a capacity crowd and all the people smiling and enjoying what she had to say. Then she could turn to Jesus and say, "Thank You for Your help," and see herself walk off, hand-in-hand with Jesus. This little prayer exercise would have an enormous effect on her outer poise in any public performance.

I shared with her how I went through these steps to remove a fear when I was working in surgery. For ten years I had an uncontrollable fear of neurosurgeons. This fear stemmed from several frightening experiences in my nurse's training. In retrospect I realize the fear, like most of our fears, was greatly magnified by my own imagination.

I remember watching my first brain operation. As a student nurse I stood swathed in a long, sterile gown with long, heavy sleeves, a sterile mask on my face, and a cap covering my hair. Excited and afraid, I wondered if I could tolerate seeing someone's brain thus exposed. My instructor whispered and motioned for me to enter the room. The room was dark. The surgeon, a famous doctor from Germany, had a light beaming over his shoulder upon the incision.

*Oh, dear,* I thought. *I wonder who the patient is. I wonder what it feels like to have your brain exposed.* I felt myself growing hot.

The surgeon bellowed, "Who are all these people in the room?"

The instructor explained, "We have two nursing students to observe today, sir."

"Why wasn't I asked before time?" he demanded.

I felt unwanted and in the way, and guilty that I was bothering him.

He shouted something at the scrub nurse (the nurse who stands shoulder to shoulder with the doctor and hands him his instruments). She handed him an instrument. He slapped it back on her tray, muttering something else in his strong German accent. Though I couldn't understand a word he said, I began to feel embarrassed for the nurse.

*How does she know what those guttural sounds mean?* I wondered. *I hope I don't ever have to be a scrub nurse for him. He'd never get the right instrument!*

The room was dark, warm, and crowded. I felt faint. He held up a tissue-mass imprisoned in his forceps.

"Do you know what I have here?" he asked me in words I didn't understand.

"I beg your pardon, sir?"

"What's the matter with you? Don't you know anything?"

"Sir, I'm sorry. I didn't understand you!" I stammered.

"Never mind!" he grunted and mumbled something about the low-grade mentality of young nurses.

From then on, I was afraid of neurosurgeons. Later, while working as a surgical nurse, I sometimes needed to scrub for brain surgeons. I faced each time with tormenting fear. Deeply imbedded in my subconscious by a strong emotional experience was the "fact" (true or not) that neurosurgeons are temperamental and difficult to understand. I dreaded these neurosurgical assignments.

"Perky," the supervisor said one day, "tomorrow you will scrub for a carotid endarterectomy and two craniotomies with Drs. MacDonald and Rivers."

Most of the nurses had difficulty understanding Dr. MacDonald. He spoke very softly into his face mask which muffled his voice even further. If a nurse couldn't understand what he was asking for, how could she give him the proper instrument? He became most upset if he had to repeat his request.

That afternoon I picked the instruments for the surgery and prepared them for sterilization. Then I studied his unique procedure. I didn't sleep well that night. Lying in bed, I prayed that God would see me through the next day. The patient's welfare was at stake! As I prayed, I asked Jesus to stand by my side. Imagining him going into the operating room with me, I prayed for him to stand there as I unwrapped the instruments. He "watched" me prepare the Mayo stand, and gown and glove the surgeon. I saw myself doing it with joy and confidence. I knew that Dr. MacDonald, Jesus, and I were working as a team to make this lady feel better.

*Imagery in Prayer*

I "saw" myself hand each instrument to Dr. MacDonald as I anticipated his need. In my prayer, I went through the entire surgery, smoothly and without fumbling. That was my request to Jesus.

The next day I reenacted my prayer in the operating room. The patient came in. Briefly I chatted with her. She showed me her flaccid, limp arm. Her words were slurred and her leg was weak. Although her problem was a little different, she looked like a patient who'd had a brain hemorrhage or stroke. Because the main blood vessel to the right side of the brain was lined with hardened minerals called plaque, sufficient blood was not reaching the brain cells. Deprived of nutrients the cells were losing their ability to function, causing a slight paralysis so the patient couldn't talk or walk or use her arm properly. As I spoke with her, I felt myself loving her, reaching out to her, and caring about her. I asked God to guide us all.

When Dr. MacDonald came into the room, I gowned and gloved him and set my Mayo stand in position. It was time for surgery to begin. He lifted his hand; I placed the scalpel in it.

He lifted his hand again. Before he could ask, I placed a hemostat in it, then another, then another. He extended his hand again. In it I placed a sponge. Then another scalpel. He was entering another layer of tissue. Dr. MacDonald went through the entire surgical procedure without asking for one instrument. If a nurse can anticipate what the physician needs before he asks, it saves him time. This is the ultimate experience for a scrub nurse. But greater than that, I didn't have to decipher his mumbling!

When the surgery was over, I leaned over and whispered in the patient's ear, "Can you move your arm now?"

She was completely awake. She squeezed my hand, then lifted her arm.

"Look," she said, "I can lift my arm! Look at my hand move. Look at my leg move! I'm healed! It's a miracle! I'm healed! Oh, doctor, thank you . . . thank you! And nurse, thank you."

I smiled and prayed, "And God, thank You!" My eyes were brimming with tears. Just then Dr. MacDonald came to me and whispered, "Did you enjoy helping in this surgery?" I nodded yes. His eyes smiled and he said, "I've never had a smoother operation."

Through prayer God had removed my fear, leaving room for full compassion toward the patient. In turn, I had received Dr. MacDonald's humaneness. Happy are the merciful for they shall obtain mercy.

After telling my story, I turned to Mrs. Winters and said, "God can help you with your fear, too. Pray and prepare. Prepare and pray!"

*Forgiveness Is Energy*

Fear is crippling; so is resentment. When we harbor resentments, we have not been merciful to others in our mind. We need to turn our resentments into forgiveness. Forgiveness is a powerful form of energy. It can be radiated to the person one resents and healing miracles can happen without a word being spoken.

When my oldest son turned sixteen, we gave him a set of

keys to the car. That was mistake number one! Being somewhat mentally gifted, he didn't have to study much to squeeze through his exams. He was alive and thrilled with living, but suddenly his priorities were vastly different from ours. I didn't know what was happening to my "darling son." On one weekend, it happened. We became total strangers. I didn't think this would ever happen in our family. After all, wasn't his father a minister? Spiritually we knew how to train our children. And wasn't his mother a nurse? Hadn't she studied psychology? Physically and psychologically we could rear our children with modern know-how.

The very thing about which we had counseled so many parents with troubled teenagers was now happening to us. His life became fast cars, girl friends (a different one every day it seemed), apathy toward church and school, and who knows what else? He and his friends were constantly working to make their cars go faster and sound louder. I remember awaking in the middle of the night, terrorstricken that he might be in trouble. I cried! I screamed to God to *do something!*

Month after month, year after year, Rusty's behavior toward his family became aloof or worse yet, rude. But this was never going to happen to my Rusty and me. I wasn't going to let the "generation gap" ruin our family. Now I was powerless! Six weeks before graduation he dropped out of school. He even left home for awhile to live with a "buddy." My heart was breaking. *He's wasting that great mind of his,* I thought.

It took tremendous courage to lead women's meetings and spiritual life retreats with the living ghost of an eighteen-year-old broken dream.

*Mercy Restores Relationships*

One day I heard Larry Christenson talk on "Forgiveness." He spoke of "unilateral forgiveness," the act we do after God forgives us; we turn around and forgive someone who has wronged us. He spoke of the enormous power in forgiveness. It mends, heals, and straightens out broken relationships. His formula was to:

1) Isolate a resentment.

2) Ask God to forgive you for the thing you have done that someone else is now doing to you. Pray, "God, judge me for a time in my life that I may have done the very same act to another person."

3) When you know God has forgiven you, radiate that forgiveness to the person who has hurt you.

Searching my mind for any hidden animosities, I couldn't think of anyone I resented. Just then I heard the bloodcurdling screech of the brakes on my son's car. I tensed.

"Oh, no! Rusty's home! I have just cleaned the house. I know he'll make it dirty! Sandy and Doug are peaceful and happy. I know he'll start a fight!"

I had isolated my animosity. For the first time in several years I became aware that I was harboring resentment toward my own son. My motherly love had so cleverly covered it up, but now my own tension pointed to a cause! I prayed, "God, forgive me for any time in my life that I brought chaos into a peaceful situation." Immediately I could remember at least three distinct times in my life as a teenager when I deliberately started trouble in a peaceful family situation because everything was running too smoothly. Vividly, I recalled my inner feelings of conflict and unrest in those days. Obnoxious behavior was a result. I prayed again, "Oh, dear God, how sorry I am I brought such misery to family members because of my own troubled soul. Now, please forgive Rusty and radiate Your forgiveness through me to him."

I could hear Rusty open the back door, walk through the back hallway, and open the kitchen door. Looking up at him I thought, *Oh Rusty, dear, I know how you feel inside. I forgive you and I know it's only temporary.*

Then I smiled and said out loud to him, "Hi, Russ!"

He was looking at the floor. I hadn't seen the whites of his eyes for six months. When I spoke, he briefly looked up at me, then down at the floor again. Then he looked up a second time and a great big grin came across his face.

"Oh, hi, mom."

He walked into the dining room. To a casual observer it may have been an uneventful greeting between mother and son. But to Rusty and me it was the dynamic moment that began the miracle of healing our deeply broken relationship. As we grew, bit by bit, to like each other again, we learned more about the power of forgiveness and mercy.

Rusty went back to finish high school and then on to college. Today he stands tall in stature and dignity. With God as his co-partner he's working toward his life goal of being everything God wants him to be. Emptied of resentments, I had room for mercy.

The fifth principle for successful business says to be kind, honest but firm. In the Sermon on the Mount Jesus said the same thing, "Blessed are the merciful, for they shall obtain mercy." This Christlike goal for personality growth will give efficacy to prayer. We must beware of the enemies of Two-way Prayer: fear, vindictiveness, and resentment.

The next Beatitude is possibly the most subtly discriminating key to determining whether the answer we get in Two-way Prayer is from God or our own conscious mind. In the next chapter we will consider our ulterior motives.

# 9

# *At Central Control*

The reason 90 percent of the people come to a Two-way Prayer Seminar is to learn how they can "see God." In the following Beatitude we find the core of Christianity:

Blessed are the pure in heart: for they shall see God.

It has been said before that "heart" in the Bible means "mind." Many times and in many ways we are told where true Christianity is lived. It is lived in the mind. Where is the mind? I believe it is in every cell of the body. Every cell of the body has memory and intelligence. Within each cell is a nucleus containing chromosomes, enzymes, minerals, electrical energy, and a multitude of chemicals. Life lies within the cellular structure.

## At the Control Center

One of the best ways to understand the human mind is to see how the central control center, the brain, functions. In *The Psychology of Jesus and Mental Health* Dr. Raymond Cramer describes it thus:

If the surface of the brain were spread out flat, it would be the size of the average front page of a newspaper. Scientists estimate that there are some thirteen billion or more brain cells . . . five times more cells in this tiny structure than the total population of the world! From the brain itself a thick white cable of nerve fibers moving down in the direction of the spinal cord forms a direct communication through some eighty-six nerve trunks like a huge network of telephone wires connecting even the remotest part of the body with operational headquarters . . . the brain! This is one of the most elaborate communication systems ever devised by which the brain keeps in constant touch with all that is going on. Only God could create such a fantastic, complex mechanism and place it in such a small area. . . .

During a lifetime there can be stored in our brain ten times more information than is contained in the nine million volumes of the Library of Congress. . . .

The brain needs more rest than any other part of our body. The energy which causes the brain cells to survive and its batteries to recharge is mainly derived from a sugar substance which has to be provided in exact amounts. The brain receives advance notice of pending trouble and is given a steady flow of information about current sugar levels. If there is too little, the liver is instructed to release the proper amount of reserve sugar.

There is a special mechanism called the blood-brain barrier which screens out substances harmful to the brain. The tragedy is that certain gases, some medications and, especially, alcohol pass through the barrier and many of these can do irreparable damage to the delicate brain cells. *However, the most damaging factors not controlled by the blood-brain barrier are the thoughts that represent various sick emotional reactions.*[1]

Our minds might be likened to an automobile engine. The oil gets dirty and needs to be changed. We do things wrong and have a guilty conscience. We need to clear the conscience, to cleanse and purify it. Sometimes our minds "need an oil change."

We can learn to keep our human machine finely tuned and balanced by checking our thoughts, ulterior motives, and drives. Frequent self-evaluation will keep us singing and humming and soaring the way God intended us to do. The psalmist cries out, "Search me, O God, . . . and know my thoughts [mind]: and see if there be any wicked way [ulterior motives] in me" (Ps. 139:23, 24).

## Pure Thoughts and Right Motives

Pure thoughts and right motives bring health to a society. Emerson said, "Spiritual force is stronger than material; thoughts rule the world." Thoughts eventually grow into actions. Marcus Antonius said, "The happiness of your life depends on the quality of your thoughts." If you're not happy today, it's your own fault. Donald Brandt says it this way, "Think exquisitely and you'll live exquisitely."

The word "pure" in the sixth Beatitude is derived from a root word meaning "to cleanse." In Two-way Prayer when we examine our conscious and subconscious desires, feelings, thoughts, emotions, purposes, and endeavors, we can test them to find out how "exquisite" they are before God. We can ask him if he approves. That way we can crosscheck our motives. Sometimes God tells us if our conscious mind has "slipped in" an ulterior motive.

I recall an occasion when I became excited about a creative idea I received for our church. When I took it back into Two-way Prayer a second time to ask God if this was what he really wanted, I "felt" him smiling and saying, "Perky, you know better than that!" Then the ulterior motive blinked as bright as a neon sign! I told him I was sorry and dismissed the portion of the idea that would benefit my personal convenience.

*Seeing God in Two-way Prayer*

The rewards of a pure mind are "they shall see God." It is a promise for today. I believe it means perceiving God through our thought processes. Based on research in the crowded tenement district of New York City and extensive research in imagery done by J. H. Schultz, neurologist and psychiatrist, we conclude that when we "see" God with our mind's eye during Two-way Prayer, the entire body and personality will react as if we had seen him in the flesh. We see him in the world around us and the things he created; we see him active in the lives of others. As we look at others and look for Christlike characteristics, regardless of how obscure they may be, it only reflects to us our own Christlike traits. This recognition strengthens that characteristic in ourselves. It is a scientific fact that we cannot see in others personality traits we do not possess ourselves. Every character trait, good or bad, is a reflection of our own selves. The characteristic we reinforce the most governs what we'll eventually become.

Someone may say, "One person I don't want to become like when I get older is my mother-in-law!" If a person says that constantly, chances are when she grows older, she *will* become exactly like her mother-in-law. She has spent years identifying the exact behavior traits she didn't like. She watched them so long that she became more and more like them.

On the other hand, if we constantly feed our minds the qualities of God which we see in others, we will become like those qualities. Albert Einstein said, "The thoughts in our subconscious set up a magnetic force field to attract or direct us to that which we desire or fear the strongest." The wise man said, "As (a man) thinketh in his heart, so is he" (Prov. 23:7).

## Results of Seeing God

Our Christianity lives, grows, and thrives in a mind free of a critical attitude toward ourselves and others. The treasured qualities of true Christianity begin with an internal sensitivity to God. I have known people with a giant of a God in them because they made room for him. They cleared away the debris of hateful emotions and filled their thoughts with love and understanding for others. As I observed these spiritual giants, I found that sometimes, contrary to my old, fixed ideas of what a true Christian should be, they struggled with exterior problems—problems like smoking, divorce, and inconsistent church attendance.

I've worked with all "kinds" of Christians for twenty-two years, day after day, in the churches my husband and I served. I love the Christian who has the discipline not to smoke, or has held his family together faithfully, and is consistent in church attendance. But I have learned that this person is not necessarily "seeing God." Such a person may be critical every moment he is in church. He may have deep, unresolved resentments toward his wife and children. Though he may not smoke, he may eat excessively or spend money selfishly while he votes down any new plans for church development.

On the other hand, when I learned to look past the external and into the fruit of one's personality, I found the "pure in mind" people were those who didn't have ulterior motives. They were single-minded, and their words were wise and kind. Gentle in their judgments of others, they saw and respected the potential of God in others. Oh, one more thing—they have a joyful, spontaneous laugh!

There is an adversary that will cloud our vision of God, and it is wrong motive. Some people call this enemy ulterior motive. We need to beware of his subtle intrusions.

To understand is to love; to love is to understand. Where there is misunderstanding, a peacemaker brings understanding. Jesus said:

"Blessed are the peacemakers: for they shall be called the children of God."

## Peacemakers within

In making peace within ourselves, we need to bring all six levels of the mind into agreement, including not only 1) the five senses, 2) the conscious mind, 3) the subconscious mind, 4) the superconscious, but, also 5) the Christ-conscious mind and 6) the God-conscious mind.

We become disturbed and confused when we do not understand our conflicting feelings. Those conflicts may come between any two levels of the mind. We need to get three handles on our lives:

1) Understand our fellowman
2) Understand ourselves
3) Understand God

God is eager to bring peace between two people if we will allow him to do so. I recall a lady in our church. Though she was a lovely and talented woman, she caused a perplexing problem. She had a charming personality and loved being involved in innovative programs. Yet, about every four to six weeks she seemed to undergo a personality change. When the schedule was running smoothly but busily, Sarah would subtly go to one person, whom I'll call Connie, and say something like, "I really don't know why JoAnn doesn't like you. I think you're so much fun."

Surprised and defensive, Connie might answer, "Oh, well, who cares about JoAnn!"

Then Sarah would whisper to JoAnn, "I can't understand Connie. She's so nice to your face but she doesn't hesitate to let people know she doesn't care about you!"

Sarah would sometimes involve three or four people, pitting one against the other. We all loved Sarah but became exasperated with her. Many times we would be unaware of her personality quirk until the destructive work was past repair.

During Two-way Prayer one day, Sarah came to mind. I prayed, "Lord, what can I do about Sarah? I can't take her off the committee. She loves the involvement, and when she is good, she's very good! But I can't let her stir up all this trouble. Should I go to her and let her know she can't cause such strife between friends?"

"Perky," he said, "Sarah has only one older brother. He is seven years older than she, and she has been like an only child. She has been accustomed to a lot of attention at home. Even though she spends most of her time at church, she still craves attention. She is mature enough to work parallel with many others for awhile, but every several weeks she has a deep driving need to be the very center of attention."

"What can I do to help her?"

"When you see her starting to cause friction between friends, think of a creative and positive way to shower her with attention. Make her the center!"

I sat silently in the presence of God for the next ten minutes. After ending my prayer, I began to do my housework. All at once a flood of ideas came to mind as to how I could make Sarah the center of attention. We gathered all her friends, and a few enemies, and took her out to lunch. We called it "Be-nice-to-Sarah day"! Another time I sent a bouquet of rosebuds to her office with a card that read, "You're one of the blossoms in God's bouquet!" These efforts paid off beautifully. Love in the committee grew strong and Christ's work went forward as Sarah's personal need was met. God helps us bring peace to our fellowman. Yet we also need to be peacemakers within ourselves.

A woman found that peace. She was beautiful but she was torn within herself. It was late one night after an all-day seminar. I was in bed but not asleep when the phone rang in the motel room.

"I know it's late but can I talk to you for a little while? It's about Two-way Prayer."

I reassured the caller I counted it a privilege to talk to her. Soon she was knocking on the door. "I can't get my prayer experience out of my mind since you led us through it this afternoon." There stood a sharp blonde woman in her early thirties. I remembered seeing her in the audience. She stood out in the crowd of 300 as a striking and exquisitely dressed woman.

"Tell me your experience," I urged.

"You told us to imagine ourselves traveling back in time two thousand years ago, and to see ourselves walking through the streets of Jerusalem looking for Jesus. Remember, you said to walk in the narrow brick streets and see a crowd ahead, then to visualize that in the center of the crowd was Jesus. You told us to work our way through the crowd until we came to him. And then you went on and led us to the end of the prayer.

"Well, I never saw a brick road. I saw myself dressed in dirty rags out in an open dirt road that led nowhere. When I saw the crowd, I knew everyone was seeing Jesus, but I couldn't see him. I walked up to the crowd but Jesus disappeared."

I asked her how she felt dressed in dirty rags on a dirt road. She told me she felt ashamed and poor. The dirt road was leading nowhere, she felt. I asked her if there was something in her life now that was making her feel ashamed.

She began to cry as she shared several traumatic experiences with me. In the past three months her husband had said he no longer loved her and wanted a divorce; she had been fired from a job she'd had for the past five years; and a special research project she had worked on for three years was rejected.

I explained that the symbols the Spirit of God gave her in prayer were speaking to her.

"But why didn't I see Jesus when I knew others in the crowd were seeing him?" she asked.

"Is Jesus real in your life?"

"No, I guess not."

"Have you ever told him you wanted him to be real in your life . . . to be a part of you, to guide and protect you?"

"No, I never did!"

I asked her if she wanted to do it now. She did. We bowed our heads and prayed together.

## Princesses Don't Wear Rags!

Before she left, we talked about the dirty ragged dress. We both realized the rags corresponded to her self-image. I suggested that she try to forget the rejection and failures of marriage and profession, but rather draw closer to Christ so that she could get a clear concept of her true worth. I told her that when she received Christ, she became a child of the King! She was a princess now!

Even though she had failed in marriage and in her work, it did not mean her world was falling apart. She was not a total failure in life. God loved her with an everlasting love. He would help her grow as a person; he would lead her to discover some worthwhile attributes and strengths she had never known she possessed.

When she found peace with God, she asked him to forgive her failures. She was instantly in close communion with him, walking a "road" that lead to joy, fulfillment, and a happy life. In this one prayer she made peace two ways. One, she made peace with God; and two, she made peace with herself. She learned the seventh Beatitude through experience: "Blessed are the peacemakers: for they shall be called the children of God."

With God as her heavenly Father, a whole new world of understanding was opened to her. With God as her guide and comfort, she has a means by which to pick up the broken pieces of her life and make something beautiful of her remaining years. She would still face difficulties, but as she learned to be persistent, God would teach her creative ways to handle her disappointments. Disappointments can be turned to victories. "Scars can be turned to stars," says Dr. Robert Schuller.

In her Two-way Prayer experiences it will be absolutely necessary for her to maintain this principle of being a peacemaker. If she allows the enemies of Two-way Prayer, troublemaking and strife, to enter her thoughts and behavior, she will find Two-way Prayer impossible. If she truly understands the living principle of the last Beatitude, she will be determined to overcome self-defeating thoughts.

The last Beatitude promises:

"Blessed are they which are persecuted for righteousness' sake: for theirs is the kingdom of heaven."

For many people this Beatitude seems to apply only to the martyrs of old. They suffered pain and abuse for living as Christians. Some were thrown to the lions, and some were burned. When we think of persecution today, we think of the Christians in Russia. It is hard to think how "persecuted for righteousness' sake" could possibly relate to Two-way Prayer.

*Pursuing and Enduring*

In the Jerusalem Bible the Beatitude is stated, "Happy are those who are persecuted in the cause of righteousness." The American Heritage Dictionary gives the meaning for persecuted as "to pursue." Thus, we can think of Jesus' teaching as "Happy are those who pursue in the cause of righteousness." As Christians we need to be dedicated and not to give up. It is one of the principles of success. This Beatitude is a lesson in endurance.

What in our life of religious freedom do we need to overcome? We need to overcome our own negative self-concepts for one thing—our faulty, self-abasing, subconscious programming that says, "You never do anything the way it should be done," or, "Others are better at it than you are," or "God is punishing you because of past sins."

The woman who "saw" herself in rags will have to "pursue" the new and true concept of herself. She is a child of God, the daughter of the King! Princesses don't wear rags. When her own accusing thoughts harass her like persecutors saying, "You're a failure in marriage" or "You're a failure in your job," she can answer with Hebrews 11:34—"Out of weakness were made strong." I have God's help now. I will be strong. I'm not a failure! I've learned valuable lessons. Now I'll know what not to do next time. I'm stronger than ever! I'm beautiful! I'm a child of God!

The promises of God are strong positives to conquer our negatives. There are many rewards for conquering, for pursuing, for overcoming. In the first place, we will get what we want if we persist long enough. It is a law of the secular world as well as the spiritual. In the second place, we enjoy a closeness with Christ who said, "I will let everyone who conquers sit beside me on my throne, just as I took my place with my Father on his throne when I had conquered" (Rev. 3:21 LB). "Happy are those who pursue in the cause of righteousness: theirs is the kingdom of heaven." Our kingdom is with the King. He lives within us.

In successful Two-way Prayer this principle is most important. Anyone can practice Two-way Prayer, but not everyone can enjoy it. Each one of these eight Beatitudes must be working in a person's life to bring about profitable prayer. Numerous verses in the Bible give clues to successful praying. Each clue, or its counterpart, will be identical to one of these Beatitudes. "Pursuing in the cause of righteousness" may have to be applied to a student of prayer who is easily defeated.

One student who was not easily defeated was a depressed businessman who had been fighting the threat of bankruptcy for a year. His wife came to a class and later at home shared her enthusiasm for Two-way Prayer with him. He came to the next seminar in a highly skeptical mood. After sitting erratically through the six sessions, he was convinced the teachings were true. He said he needed to take the course again to hear, now, what I had said. God revealed to this man a striking truth about himself while he was going through a prayer exercise. Although this businessman was a Christian, a beautiful new concept of God's love worked a miraculous healing in his troubled, failure-prone mind. By the end of the seminar, exciting business proposals were being pursued that prevented bankruptcy.

The blessings from the second seminar were great. Eight months later, he enrolled in the seminar a third time. He said he needed reinforcement. His Two-way Prayer times at home were hitting some "dry spells." The third time through the course gave him such in-depth knowledge and prayer experience that the blessings began to flow daily. It has been a year and a half and he is now teaching others the art and joy of Two-way Prayer. He pursued prayer. Today he walks hand-in-hand with God, having a daily dialogue with the one of whose presence he believed he was not worthy. Because of his persistence, he found success in business and in prayer.

Too many people don't persist when the hurdles of persecution are placed in their way. They let defeat spoil an exciting discovery. Theirs is never the kingdom of heaven.

# 10

# *This Is Your World:*
# *Get into It*

"A physicist has said there is enough atomic energy in one person to blow up the city of New York." [1] If we have enough energy to be that destructive, what can we do for *good!* We are making our mark in the world moment by moment, day by day.

From the time you were born, you've played center stage in your world. You are the main actor and you are affecting thousands of lives by the way you act and react. Lying dormant in your life are gifts and treasures the world has yet to see. No one can do—or give, or create—in quite the way you can!

On the day you were born the world had a look at your style— that of a champion. You were born with the taste of victory in your mouth. Your very physical existence makes you a miracle to behold! Imagine, if you can, the state of Texas covered with silver dollars one hundred yards thick (the length of a football field). Imagine someone's mixing one silver dollar painted red in this vast area. The chances of your finding that one red coin would be better than your chances were of ever being born.

At that given moment of your birth, you overcame the greatest crisis you'll ever have to face in life. Actually, that enormous crisis was threefold: physical, psychological, and sociological.

In your mother's lifetime, nature directed her to produce some 500 microscopic cells called ovum. The egg-cell, or ovum, is unique. It is the most intricate and beautiful component of God's highest creation, for it is the beginning of human life. At one time you were no more than one little egg-cell! But what an important cell that was.

Each egg-cell is important, for it carries all the physical characteristics of your parents, grandparents, great-grandparents—all the way back to the beginning of man. Each month an egg-cell is produced, ready to burst into the life of a complete human being. But usually the magic of full life doesn't happen. In fact, if a mother gives birth to three children, that means 497 egg-cells never grow into human beings. Now you were one out of 500 that made it. That's tremendous!

It is even more wonderful to consider the quality and power you received from your father. As you were delicately being formed, the precise timing was extremely important. Out of centuries of time into the narrow confines of your parents' life span, there were only 48 hours in one given month that you, the little egg-cell, could be fertilized by the infinitesimal male sperm. At a specific hallowed moment a mass of sperm numbering from 60 to 150 million cells was released. From that multitude of male cells, only the fastest, the strongest, and the most diligent cell, overcoming tremendous obstacles, was the first to reach the ovum—and it won triumphantly! That victorious sperm left millions behind—and you were marvelously begun!

Psychologically, too, you were a winner. After nine months of the most perfect environment the human being may ever experience, you were forced out into a terrifying experience of separation, harsh light, noise, roughness, and cold. The memory of this experience fades, but it is never lost entirely.

Experiments have been done under local anesthesia to stimulate brain cells to bring back a vivid memory. Repeated cases tell about patients' recalling such catastrophic events that they ask for the tests to be stopped. The memory is one of being flushed down a dark canal, or of swirling waters suffocating the patient. Some authorities believe this is related to repetitious dreams of the "drainage pipe" [2] or being "flushed down a toilet." They feel this could represent the infant memory of the journey through the birth canal. As traumatic and smashing as that was to your psyche or soul, you were able to overcome it, to grow, to develop, to learn, to go on.

You really deserve a gold medal for the victory socially. On the day you were to be born you had no orientation, no instruction book on how to get out of there, no red flashing signs saying "exit." You had to figure it all out yourself. And when you finally found your way by yourself, did anyone say, "How smart you are to be born so well!"? No! Some doctor probably picked you up by the ankles, turned you upside down, and spanked your sociologically tender posterior. You were born into a room of total strangers and absolutely nude!

Not only were you stripped of all dignity but you really were not very pretty! Your hair was a disaster! It was uncombed and smeared with vernix—a white, waxy, gunky substance that is very difficult to wash off. You didn't give your new acquaintances a beautiful smile either. You were frowning, squinty-eyed, and you squeaked. How would you like a rerun of *that* experience in your adult life?

No matter how many embarrassing moments you think you have experienced as an adult, you will never have to endure such an embarrassing moment again. It didn't demolish you. You have made it through all that and unleashed your energy on the world. God didn't place you on this earth to struggle and squirm in defeat and weakness. Quite the contrary. You were born a champion. If you are weak and defeated, you've done it to yourself, but you can change.

Life's most fascinating experiences are within the reach of every man, woman, and child. An abundant life can flow from the core of a God-centered mind to every cell of one's body. Power and energy enough to blow up the city of New York can be turned inward in Two-way Prayer. This will enable us to "see God," giving us a life of glistening hope.

Over twenty million Americans are suffering from emotional disorders, we are told. Nine million are severely disturbed and are walking our streets, rubbing shoulders with us. Tension affects us all with varying degrees of destruction. Nearly every person has heard echoes of the mind say, "Who in this life can I trust?" "Why can't I be the person I want to be?" "Is this all there is to life?" Fatigue, boredom, and anger stifle the thoughts of joy, strength, and peace. Yet why should we submit to becoming a humanoid of society, an empty shell, a robot? Why should we be content to live only part of our lives, unfulfilled and drab?

## Life's Fascinating Experiences

When we began this race, we were champions. It is possible to be faithful and persevere to the end. We will finish life's race as the champions God intended us to be. It is never too late to try. Defeat and discouragement have taught us all valuable lessons. We can build on past failures and become stronger than ever for having overcome. God created us with the power and the means to reach our God-centered conscious minds. There we find comfort, healing, and instruction. Surrounded with the Bible's promises and strength from God, we can probe through the barriers that keep us from the sixth level of the mind, the God-consciousness which releases to the world the awesome, loving power of God within us.

If we should find there is friction and bickering in our lives, we have done it to ourselves. We can readily pinpoint the need to adjust our attitudes by comparing our thoughts with the thoughts of Jesus.

One dynamically effective exercise is to reconstruct our inner world through Two-way Prayer. The secret lies in the use of the condensed simplicity of the Beatitudes.

## Eight Exercises for Spiritual Equilibrium

In any of the exercises below we can find the questions to ask and the promises to be granted. If we have not been "seeing" God, for example, and feel the lack, the question in exercise 6 forces us to examine our motives before God. In like manner, we can rebuild our souls through the use of the other exercises.

### Exercise #1
*Matthew 5:3:* "Blessed are the poor in spirit: for theirs is the kingdom of heaven."

\* \* \*

Have we been successful but not arrogant? Then ours is the power within.

\* \* \*

Business says: Your attitude should be successful but not arrogant of mind.

* * *

Enemy to Two-way Prayer: Arrogance.

*Exercise #2*
*Matthew 5:4:* "Blessed are they that mourn: for they shall be comforted."

* * *

Have we been sorry for the wrong in our lives? Then we will receive comfort and renewed strength and energy.

* * *

Business says: Deal with your problems, don't bury them.

* * *

Enemy to Two-way Prayer: Negative emotion.

*Exercise #3*
*Matthew 5:5:* "Blessed are the meek: for they shall inherit the earth."

* * *

Have we been gentle and well-disciplined in response to the commands of God? Then we will have what we desire, even the earth.

* * *

Business says: Be mentally strong and self-disciplined.

* * *

Enemy to Two-way Prayer: Procrastination.

*Exercise #4*
*Matthew 5:6:* "Blessed are they which do hunger and thirst after righteousness: for they shall be filled."

* * *

Do we long to be just and good, seeking to follow the new nature of God within us rather than our base, negative drives? Then we will be totally fulfilled.

* * *

Business says: Believe in your inner self; it is powerful.

* * *

Enemy to Two-way Prayer: Apathy and indifference.

*Exercise #5*
*Matthew 5:7:* "Blessed are the merciful: for they shall obtain mercy."

\* \* \*

Have we been gracious and merciful? Then that is what life will return to us.

\* \* \*

Business says: Be kind and honest, fair but firm.

\* \* \*

Enemy to Two-way Prayer: Vindictiveness, resentment and fear.

*Exercise #6*
*Matthew 5:8:* "Blessed are the pure in heart: for they shall see God."

\* \* \*

Have our minds and motives been pure? Then we "shall see God."

\* \* \*

Business says: Keep your thoughts and drives pure. Have frequent times for self-evaluation. Check your motives constantly.

\* \* \*

Enemy to Two-way Prayer: Wrong motives.

*Exercise #7*
*Matthew 5:9:* "Blessed are the peacemakers: for they shall be called the children of God."

\* \* \*

Have we made peace within ourselves and with others, and with God? Then we will be called the sons and daughters of God.

\* \* \*

Business says: Be known as a man of your word. Where there is misunderstanding, bring understanding. Be a peacemaker.

\* \* \*

Enemy to Two-way Prayer: Troublemaking and strife.

*Exercise #8*
*Matthew 5:10:* "Blessed are they which are persecuted for right-eousness' sake: for theirs is the kingdom of heaven."

* * *

When persecution and difficulties hinder our progress in pursuing the cause of right, do we wither and give up? If we pursue we will experience power and beauty within our souls.

* * *

Business says: Be dedicated—don't give up.

* * *

Enemy to Two-way Prayer: Defeat.

*Reconstructing the Inner World*

When a motor is running smoothly, there is no need to think about it. If it begins to vibrate or sound strange, it becomes necessary to stop and take a look at the trouble spot. Sometimes the motor needs tuning. The first indication that something is spiritually off balance may be a dull or empty feeling when we pray. We might feel that "God is far away"—as David felt. Then it is time to examine the soul to see if any of the inner tormentors have taken up residence in the conscious mind. Some of these inner tormentors are:

| | |
|---|---|
| Arrogance | Wrong motives |
| Negative Emotion | Troublemaking |
| Procrastination | Strife |
| Self-will | Anxiety |
| Apathy | Fatigue |
| Vindictiveness | Inferiority |
| Resentment | Loneliness |
| Fear | Bashfulness |

All of these enemies will muddy the windows of the soul. It will become difficult to see the reflection of Christ clearly; then we experience confusion and aimless dissatisfaction. After taking an inventory of the soul, one or two enemies may be identified. The following steps help in dealing with these tormentors!

1) *Confess our sin.* The first step is to confess our sin to Christ. If the weakness is imbedded deeply in the mind and personality, a more drastic step is needed.

2) *We should command the negative to leave,* and in the name of Jesus Christ redirect that energy to its counterpart.

3) *Visualize the negative emotion.* This process is beautifully effective if one can visualize the negative emotion. See the emotion as a person. Arrogance, for example, may have a top hat, tuxedo, walking cane, and white gloves. He may be walking with his eyebrows raised and nose in the air. One may see this image as a part of his personality. Knowing that God wants one to achieve but not with arrogance, it becomes necessary to convert arrogance to humility.

4) *See him leave.* In prayer, one could say, "Lord, You have my best interest at heart. You have told me not to be arrogant or haughty, for my own personal growth. Therefore, in Your name, I command arrogance to leave." A pictorial thinker may visualize the man in the top hat crouch and run. A digital thinker will only imagine the man leaving.

5) *See his counterpart come in.* As we keep Christ present in our thoughts, Humility will walk in. Perhaps he's dressed in everyday modern clothes. He may walk up to Jesus and bow at his feet acknowledging that all he has learned, and all he has accomplished, are the result of the knowledge and power he has received from Christ. This is called attitude realignment. Christ realigns our attitude from:

| | | |
|---|---|---|
| Arrogance | to | Humility |
| Negative emotion | to | Positive thinking |
| Procrastination | to | Obedience |
| Self-will | to | God-will |
| Apathy | to | Truth-seeking |
| Vindictiveness | to | Mercifulness |
| Resentment | to | Forgiveness |
| Fear | to | Courage |
| Wrong motives | to | Singlemindedness |
| Trouble Maker | to | Peacemaker |
| Strife | to | Understanding |
| Anxiety | to | Tranquility |
| Fatigue | to | Energy |
| Inferiority | to | Worthwhileness |

| Loneliness | to | Christ's presence |
| Bashfulness | to | Confidence |

When in prayer, then, one visualizes the presence of Christ. This attitude realignment has a noticeable effect on the personality.

## Responding to Personification and Visualization

Let me share a few thoughts about the dynamic of visualization. It is a scientific process to pray by image, to "see" Christ and to walk up to him and ask for health, well-being, friendship, bodily healing or confidence. Then in faith we "see" Christ giving it to us. "See" ourselves healed; "see" ourselves achieving; "see" ourselves working hard and accomplishing our goals. Those images "lock" into the hypothalamus gland of the brain and the body must react obediently in accord with that image.

Dr. Carl Simonton, a radiation therapist in Texas, has been using imagery in his cancer research. The patients whom he trains to imagine the cancer tumors getting smaller as a supplement to radium treatment, have better results than the patients who have the radium treatment without the imagery exercises. In a symposium held at the University of California at Los Angeles in 1972, Dr. Simonton discussed also how he taught his patients the importance of having a positive attitude about life and to maintain a strong will to live. These patients enjoyed more benefits from the accepted treatment for cancer than patients who didn't keep a positive attitude.[3]

In a class given in medical schools across the nation, Dr. Barbara Brown discussed the work of Jacobson at Harvard in 1908. He noted if his subjects imagined themselves pressing a telegraph key with their middle finger, even though the finger did not move, there was recorded energy from the exact muscle groups that would have moved if the fingers had.[4]

The image locked into the hypothalamus gland (a small gland in the brain structure) is the image to which the body and personality respond. If we are ill, but deep in the inner recesses of the mind we feel we'll never get well, even though the tongue and mouth say from the conscious level of thought that we will, our recovery will be extremely slow—if we recover at all.

"Believing in your heart" as the Scriptures use the term, means, I believe, "locking it into the hypothalamus gland." Only we and God know what is *really* locked into the hypothalamus. The body and personality will act accordingly. The mouth may say something else. The mouth may say, "I like money," but locked in the hypothalamus may be the message, "Money is evil. ' The personality will show a number of self-defeating patterns that keep us from accumulating money. The powerful use of the hypothalamus is clear when we read "heart" in these scripture verses:

"If I regard iniquity in my heart [subconscious mind], the Lord will not hear me" (Ps. 66:18).

"Create in me a clean heart, O God" (Ps. 51:10).

"Out of the abundance of the heart [subconscious] the mouth speaketh" (Matt. 12:34).

"As he thinketh in his heart [hypothalamus-subconscious], so is he" (Prov. 23:7).

"That if thou shalt confess with thy mouth the Lord Jesus, and shalt believe in thine heart [subconscious] that God hath raised him from the dead, thou shalt be saved" (Rom. 10:9).

To my understanding, it is in the heart, the subconscious, locked in the hypothalamus gland, where true Christianity abounds, not in man's dogma and fixed standards for self-righteous behavior. Deep in a man's subconscious does he truly love God? Does he love himself? Does he love his neighbor?

*Locking Scripture into the Subconscious*

Here is an exercise using imagery that can be done with 1 Corinthians 13. If done daily for seven days, one will notice a sweetening effect on life. The exercise will fix the scripture emotionally in the hypothalamus.

1) Before going into Two-way Prayer, read 1 Corinthians 13: 4–8.

2) Next, read it again, replacing the word "love" with your name.

3) Read 1 Corinthians 13:4–8 three or four times with your name in it. Placing your name in the blank spaces, it will read as follows from the Living Bible!

_____ (Your name) is always patient and kind;

_____ is never jealous

_____ is never boastful

_____ is never conceited

_____ is never rude

_____ is never selfish

_____ does not take offense

_____ is not resentful

_____ takes no pleasure in other peoples' sins, but delights in the truth

_____ is always ready to excuse

_____ is always ready to trust

_____ is always ready to hope

_____ is always ready to endure whatever comes.

4) Then as we go into Two-way Prayer, we sit quietly before God. One of these phrases comes to mind. We talk it over with Christ and ask him to search our minds. Was there a time we were jealous? We ask him to forgive it, and we forgive ourselves. Seeing ourselves replacing jealousy with love in a given situation, we go on to another phrase. We may be able to pray about two or three phrases. We repeat the scripture reading the next day. The Spirit of God will bring to our thoughts the specific phrase we need to deal with each day.

One who reads the Bible before prayer finds a wealth of conversation-starters with God. Filled with delight and joy, he will become a lifetime student of prayer and Bible study. He will be on a path of intrigue and discovery as he gets to know himself, God, and others through developing an inner sensitivity of love. We develop skills in everything else. Why not develop the skill that brings life into focus—the inner sensitivity of love?

Bringing life into focus gives a contentment that, once discovered, the student of prayer does not want to lose. Yet sometimes students ask, "Why am I unable to concentrate in prayer?" Some of the reasons are:

1) Too many negative emotions.

2) Worry. Someone has defined worry as taking responsibility God never intended us to have. We worry about our kids, money, the future, what other people think, our wives, our husbands. We need to learn that regardless of outward circumstances, our inner souls are at peace with God.

3) Poor diet. We sometimes have too many refined flours and refined sugars in the diet. Refined flours and sugars are known to make a person irritable, nervous, intellectually sluggish, and paranoid. Large amounts of refined sugar have been known to cause hallucinations. Caffeine in coffee, tea, and soft drinks will stimulate artificially to keep a person from relaxation. A healthy body has an advantage in bringing harmony between mind and soul.

4) The disease called "Psycho-sclerosis." [5] "Psycho" meaning mind, and "sclerosis" meaning hardening. "Hardening of the mind" prevents us from ever knowing the many new and exciting blessings God has for us. A fixed unwillingness to change or to accept new ideas will keep us from discovering God in all his fullness. We should learn to be "wonderologists." Those who study the wonders of God are wonderologists. They will never grow old! David prayed, "Enlarge my mind that I may know you." We need to pray, "Lengthen the cords of my tent. Make the stakes stronger." The tent of my mind is getting larger to contain God in all his wonder, power, and greatness. We need to do away with the fixed, rigid walls of preconceived ideas and prejudices. Believe in ourselves. Believe in miracles. God loves the spectacular. He is spectacular. Let him prove it in our lives.

5) Adrenalin, a natural stimulant in the body, will prevent us from concentrating in Two-way Prayer. Adrenalin will flow at certain times:

a) *Times of excitement,* maybe over something good. The night before Christmas is not a good time to go into Two-way Prayer. God understands. These times are temporary. They are good times for one-way prayer.
b) *Times of deep emotional upset.* Two-way Prayer will have to wait until we work through the upset in our life. Start working it through by prayers of supplication, hymns, and Bible reading. Comfort and wisdom will quiet the soul.

### Dry Spells

Temporary periods of not being able to concentrate on prayer are normal in life. They may also be times when God is having us mark time spiritually. Sometimes I have received a flood of spiritual and creative activity during prayer. Then I experience a "dry spell." I have found these "dry spells" are just as important to my progress as the periods of illumination. I need time to carry out the ideas God has given me to work on.

Furthermore, we need time for our bodies and emotions to catch up with the spiritual growth. When the three come in balance once more, creativity will again begin to flow. Our trying to force an experience in Two-way Prayer will also foil our communication. There have been times when a student has had such an ecstatic experience that he tries to repeat it the next time he prays. Attempts such as this are common with inexperienced students of Two-way Prayer. The first encounter with Christ creates a deeply memorable experience; yet no two spiritual experiences are the same. The harder one tries to contrive an event, the more it will evade him. In trying to make something happen, we create the tension that keeps the mind from "being still."

Many find a union and a oneness with God such as they have never known. Then, for some reason, that closeness is gone. They call or write and ask me what they can do. If they do not feel as close to God today as they did yesterday, it is because *they* moved. God is still there but something has clouded *their* view.

Much like Moses at Mount Sinai, the student of prayer will find God still waiting for him at the top of the mountain. In chapters 19 and 20 of Exodus we read that the Lord called Moses up to the mountain top to speak to him. When Moses got there, God gave him instructions on two stone tablets. These instructions are called the Ten Commandments. While Moses communed with God, the people in the valley fell into sin. Moses descended the mountain.

He saw how drastically the people had sinned. In a rage of temper, he threw down the tablets of stone. They broke. The Lord God was grieved at Moses' lack of control; yet he loved Moses. So God called him to the mountain top a second time. In Exodus 24:12 God said, "I will be there" to meet you. Moses returned a second time. But this time it was a little more work for Moses. God did not provide the tablets, but rather told Moses to prepare the tablets himself by chipping away the stone (Exod. 34:1). It was a lonely journey. Moses was instructed to climb alone.

## God Waits at the Mountain Top

Once a person loses his awareness of God, it might take more work to chip away negative behavior, one piece at a time, one layer at a time back through the levels of the mind where he'll find God still waiting. It will be a lonely journey and no one can do it for him. His reward will be renewed power, understanding, and spiritual growth.

We never go backward. It may be a little harder the second time to renew that intimacy, yet because of the difficulty, we will take more care the next time to avoid, at all costs, that which spoils our sensitivity to God.

## A Five-way Test

Our sensitivity to God is important in distinguishing the answers we get in prayer. Many people ask me how they can know whether an answer is from God or if it comes from the conscious mind. Just as there are four ways to test creative ideas, there are five ways to test an answer to see if it came from God:

1) Does it "square-up" with what the Bible teaches? If the answer conflicts with biblical principles, we know there's self-involvement in the answer.

2) Will the answer be good for mankind?

3) Will the answer honor God?

4) Has it ever been done before? If our answer, to our knowledge, has never been suggested before, it is a creative idea. True creativity comes from God. He *is* creativity. "Create" is the first verb in the Bible!

5) If in doubt, we go into Two-way Prayer and ask God again. In time, one develops trust and discernment. If we follow an answer, and decide later it was our own self-answer rather than God's answer, that's good! We've learned something about ourselves. We think it through. We ask ourselves how we could have been more discerning. Review the Beatitudes. Would the answer have passed the "be" attitude test? Could we have been more perceptive? As we grow spiritually, we become more sensitive to God and to ourselves.

Although we have the innate capacity to become more sensitive, we do not use these gifts to their fullest magnitude. We use about one-fifth of our lung capacity. The heart has the ability to double its normal beat. The digestive system has the capacity to go far beyond what the body needs. The ears screen out many noises we do not want to hear; yet we hear many noises we should hear. A mother can sleep through the noise of busy traffic, radio, T.V., and railroad trains, but she will wake up at a baby's slightest whimper. We can tune-in—or tune-out!

Many people have learned how to tune-in to God's silent voice by learning the technique of Two-way Prayer. The wonder we find in those inner chambers of prayer with God awes the soul. We stand breathless at the treasures and power of prayer.

Prayer is the lover's guide; strength to the heart bowed down in grief; hope to the man not yet perfect; wisdom to the rattled and confused.

Prayer is the cup of life. Some drink deep while others die of thirst.

# Questions and Answers

The following questions or areas of concern deal with the six levels of the mind and the four states of consciousness:

*The four states of consciousness and six levels of the mind all sound exciting but they seem very complicated to me.*

I appreciate how you feel. We, in the sciences, like to make things sound difficult. The concepts in chapters 2 and 3 are not as difficult as they sound. A nodding acquaintance with these terms will help you to understand how Two-way Prayer works. You will also know what happens when prayer doesn't work.

The four states of consciousness are:
>        1) Beta
>        2) Alpha
>        3) Theta
>        4) Delta

The six levels of the mind are:
>        1) Five senses
>        2) Conscious
>        3) Subconscious
>        4) Superconscious—Genius
>        5) Christ-conscious
>        6) God-conscious

*In your Two-way Prayer classes, have there been any physical healings?*

Yes, many. The beautiful aspect of God is that during Two-way Prayer he meets each individual person at the place of his or her most basic need. Sometimes that greatest need is physical healing; sometimes, emotional; sometimes, spiritual.

After I gave the twelve-hour seminar in a Mennonite church in southern California, the church secretary called me. She was in ecstasy over the miracle God had performed in her life. Without realizing it, over a period of years she had become addicted to tranquilizers and strong sleeping pills. The gradual need for an increase in medication made her suspicious of her addiction. She went to several physicians for relief, only to be told she was "hooked." She was informed it would take at least a year of enormous self-will and discipline before she could be cured. It was her destiny to yearn constantly for the drugs.

One evening the class entered the Two-way Prayer exercise. I told them to imagine Jesus standing before them. Then I said, "Ask him about your most heartfelt need." She did. When she went home, she continued to go into the exercises of Two-way Prayer on her own. One day, during the exercise of prayer, she felt God's healing power. She waited two weeks before she called me.

"Perky," she said, "I haven't had a tranquilizer or a sleeping pill for two weeks. The miracle is that I don't even desire it! Not once, not even one time. In fact, most of the time I don't even think about it. I'm healed—completely healed!"

There have been any number of tension-related illnesses healed: backaches, colitis, ulcers, dysmennorhea, skin disease and migraine headaches—to name a few. Physical healing seems to be a side benefit of prayer.

*I can relax my body but I have a hard time quieting my thoughts. Is there a way to relax my mind?*

This is the problem of most Americans; and, incidentally, it is one of the reasons prayer can be so unfulfilling. We want to talk to God, but before long we're thinking of other things. As we relax our bodies, we need to fix our attention on something specific. At first our attention is focused on the main muscle groups of the body. With our minds, we tell our muscles to "let go" of the forehead, eyelids, and cheek muscle groups. Then other muscles follow.

When the body is relaxed, the mind needs a fixed center on which to anchor its thoughts. Fragmented ideas need to be put in order and given direction. Since the direction in prayer is God, if we think his name each time we inhale, it will discourage tangential thoughts. The mind cannot think of two things at once.

This fact can be easily demonstrated. The next time you're in a group of people, ask their cooperation. Tell them you want them to count from one to ten silently. During their counting, tell them you'll ask them their names. When you do, ask them to say their names out loud . . . everyone at once. After you've prepared them, begin the exercise. Say, "Now begin counting to yourselves from one to ten slowly." After a few seconds ask, "What is your name?" After they've given their names, ask them what happened to their counting. Invariably, they will say it ceased when they were forced to think of their names. This happens to our busy thoughts when we keep saying a specific word with each breath. In Two-way Prayer, we can use the words: Jesus, Immanuel, Messiah, or Jesus, Father, God, or simply Yahweh or God. I prefer "Jesus, Immanuel, Messiah."

*Why do you use those three words?*

1) Jesus means, "For he shall save his people from their sins."
2) Immanuel means, "God with us."
3) Messiah means, "The Promised One."

These powerful names sum up the story of God and his love for man as told in the Holy Scriptures. They are the first three names for God in the New Testament. But they serve another purpose. Those words act like a magnet drawing us to what we are saying. The very vibrations of the thought of God help us to reach the God-consciousness level of our mind. God's promise is, "And when you draw close to God, God will draw close to you" (James 4:8 LB).

*I have studied a little Freudian psychology and I'm afraid to open myself up to my subconscious.*

Many people who were followers of Freud feel that way. The truth is, we have much to thank Freud for in the field of psychology, but I certainly disagree with his teachings that the subconscious mind is something horrible. I have found it to be a marvelous tool of God to help us find our way in life. If we experience fearful, painful reflections from the subconscious, it's an indication we need to deal with those reflections. Many times we have buried negative thoughts so deeply we don't realize how physically and spiritually harmful they are to us. If we are going to have a close walk with God it's important to be at peace in the subconscious mind. If the subconscious is not at peace, we need to "clean it out."

*How do we "clean it out?"*

By getting rid of the garbage. In computer language GIGO, garbage-in—garbage-out, we need to separate the good programming from the destructive programming. Contemplating our negative emotions and giving them to Christ helps us get rid of harmful tension and to be at peace with God, ourselves, and our fellowmen. This kind of peace permeates the subconscious and the soul is tranquil.

*In what way do other people contribute to our negative concepts?*

Once we believe a faulty concept someone has taught us, we have recorded those thoughts. It may not have been true, but our entire personality reacts as if it were true. We believed them. The subconscious mind believed them.

For example, if I am told all my life that I am not worthy

of God, cannot do anything good, and am worthless, I will believe it. I will act on that negative belief. When I go into Two-way Prayer, I won't feel worthy of God's presence so my own faulty concept will keep me from feeling close to him. Before I make any more progress in prayer, I'll have to deal with that idea.

As I read the Bible, I will be reassured of how much God feels I'm worth. I may read, "For a soul is far too precious to be ransomed by mere earthly wealth. There is not enough of it in all the earth to buy eternal life for just one soul, to keep it out of hell" (Ps. 49:8,9 LB). When I recognize my mistaken idea, I will say, "Hey! I really am worth a lot to God." That's a healing thought to a troubled subconscious mind! "Blessed be the Lord God of Israel; for he has visited and redeemed his people" (Luke 1:68). The word "redeemed" means "bought." That means we are *valuable* to God!

*When you tell us to think about our negative emotions, specifically what do you mean?*

Fears and resentments mostly. Under those general categories may come jealousy, worry, inferiority, hostility, depression, sadness, loneliness, frustration, apprehension, envy, gloom, irritability, shyness, boredom, disgust, guilt, and discouragement.

*How can I be sure no emotional or spiritual harm can come to me during Two-way Prayer?*

Two-way Prayer is Christ-centered. Keeping your mind on Christ is the safety valve.

"What shall we then say to these things? If God be for us, who can be against us? He that spared not his own Son, but delivered him up for us all, how shall he not with him also freely give us all things? Who shall lay anything to the charge of God's elect? It is God that justifieth. Who is he that condemneth? It is Christ that died, yea rather, that is risen again, who is even at the right hand of God, who also maketh intercession for us. Who shall separate us from the love of Christ? Shall tribulation, or distress, or persecution, or famine, or nakedness, or peril, or sword? As it is written, For thy sake we are killed all the day long; we are accounted as sheep for the slaughter. Nay, in all these things we are more than conquerors through him that loved us. For I am persuaded, that neither death, nor life, nor angels, nor principalities, nor powers, nor things present, nor things to come, nor height, nor depth, nor any other creature, shall be able to separate us from the love of God, which is in Christ Jesus our Lord" (Rom. 8:31–39).

"Thou wilt keep him in perfect peace whose mind is stayed on thee because he trusteth in thee" (Isa. 26:3).

*Is Two-way Prayer anything like hypnosis—or self-hypnosis?*

No, not at all. The hypnotic or theta state as I use it refers to a specific brain wave pattern. I'm not referring to any commercial program used for entertainment or monetary purposes. The theta brain wave pattern, as I've explained, is normally found any time during our waking and sleeping moments. Theta is related somehow to memories, imagery, and visualization. Sometimes in prayer a person uses imagery.

*You said something about praying using imagery. Is this part of Two-way Prayer?*

Sometimes. If a person is a pictorial thinker, he may have some exquisitely beautiful experiences in Two-way Prayer. Some people don't visualize. They are called digital thinkers.

*That's interesting. I wonder what kind of thinker I am.*

Actually, there are just two kinds of thinkers: the pictorial and the digital. In a classroom I may say to twenty people, "See the boy run." Then I ask how many actually "saw" a boy run . . . saw an image as we see in our dreams? About 40 percent will raise their hands. I love to ask them to describe their "boy." One will say, "He had a red and white striped T-shirt, blue shorts, and blond hair." Another will say, "My boy had on overalls and a white shirt. He was running in the street, pulling a red wagon." At this point, the digital thinkers look wide-eyed, mouths open and chins resting on chest! They ask, "You mean those people actually saw colors? They 'see' people and things!" A digital thinker has never "seen" images in his waking hours. Pictorial thinkers "see" them often—vivid colors, vivid images. However, some pictorial thinkers "see" in black and white. Some people tell me they only see part of the boy. For instance, they see only the legs running. This is utterly fascinating to me, since I'm a digital thinker and never see such images.

*Are there advantages to being a pictorial thinker?*

Definitely yes! It takes less time and energy to be a pictorial thinker. Creative people are usually pictorial thinkers.

*What makes a person a pictorial thinker?*

Pictorial thinking is the language of the subconscious. The subconscious mind doesn't "think" in words. We have all experienced images from the subconscious during the dreaming process. The pictorial thinkers "see" the images direct from the subconscious. The digital thinkers, for some reason, have a block between the subconscious level and the conscious level of the mind. (See illustration on page 139.)

*How is this useful in Two-way Prayer?*

Mostly in understanding the experience. The pictorial thinkers will actually "see" Christ as they pray. The images of the subconscious may also occur during the quiet stage. Each of the images is significant—some more meaningful than others.

*How can a digital thinker appreciate Two-way Prayer if he doesn't visualize?*

The experience can be just as meaningful. In prayer, the digital

# ILLUSTRATION

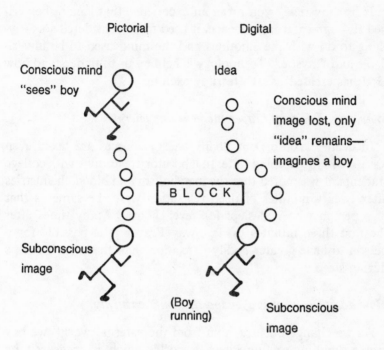

Pictorial      Digital

Conscious mind
"sees" boy

Idea

Conscious mind
image lost, only
"idea" remains—
imagines a boy

BLOCK

Subconscious
image

(Boy
running)

Subconscious
image

### Pictorial Thinkers

They don't have a visual block between the subconscious and the conscious. It takes less time and energy for creative thinking.

### Digital Thinkers

They can "imagine" a boy running, but they don't see the actual picture. They don't "see" as they do in dreams. The image works its way through the block and is "lost" to the conscious mind. Only the idea remains.

thinker develops the skill of discerning God through his thoughts and feelings.

*Isn't all this rather mystical?*

If by "mystical" you mean an experience that cannot be verified through external evidence, it used to be considered so. Anything to do with the emotions and the mind used to be unverifiable and "mystic." Technology is helping us to understand how God has created us. It's terribly exciting.

*Why does Two-way Prayer increase our energy?*

In deep relaxation our bodily energy sources are taxed even less than in the sleeping state. In laboratory tests done with college students, it was noted that the metabolism and blood chemistries after twenty minutes of deep relaxation were the same as that of a person who had slept for seven hours.[1] Many times after the first three minutes of Two-way Prayer it is possible for a person to have greater bodily relaxation than that which occurs during sleep.

*How does Two-way Prayer increase our sensitivity?*

As we change our attention from the external world, we pay more attention to our internal world which is measured by thoughts and feelings. Becoming more aware of our feelings, we become more aware of other peoples' feelings, thus more sensitive to their needs.

*How does Two-way Prayer help us gain success?*

Someone has said success is not determined by what we are but rather what we could become. I like to think of success as doing that for which we were born. This is different from prosperity. Two-way Prayer helps a person find that for which he was born by integrating his body, mind, and soul. When the search for fulfillment is done on only two levels, the mind and the body, there will be a vague discontent. We need the soul to communicate with God. He helps us find success!

*How does Two-way Prayer increase my joy?*

There is a motto hanging on the wall of our little cottage in Mexico that says, "Joy is the infallible sign of the presence of God." I have yet to find a person who has felt God's presence who didn't have joy beaming from his eyes.

*How does Two-way Prayer increase my tranquility, reduce stress, and improve physical and mental health?*

In the human body there is a protective mechanism against overstress. It is related to a chemical in the blood called lactate. Scientists feel increased blood lactate is instrumental in producing certain anxiety attacks. "Along with the drop in oxygen consumption and Alpha wave production during meditation, there is a marked decrease in blood lactate . . . blood lactate levels fall rapidly within the first ten minutes of meditation." [2] This drop in blood lactate helps to explain why medical science says meditation is the greatest cure for anxiety known today.

*You keep saying "develop the skill of Two-way Prayer." What do you mean by that?*

Jesus taught us the art of prayer. Just as in many other accomplishments, prayer requires competence. The requirements for effective prayer are simple but not easy (I say, "Not easy" because we have to train our tense bodies to relax). Our minds need a time of preparation before we are ready to pray. Prayer becomes a lifetime study of God and his law for our total happiness.

*Do you believe we can "pray without ceasing?"*

Yes, I believe every God-centered thought is a prayer. We can pray twenty-four hours a day, even in our sleep!

*How can we do that?*

By recognizing that the mind is active twenty-four hours a day, and never sleeps. It is the God-centered subconscious mind that is in constant communion with God, even though at this level the conscious mind may not be aware of such activity.

*It sounds like you're saying our subconscious mind is flashing abstract thoughts and images to our conscious mind every minute.*

That's exactly what I am saying. One source tells us these images are flashed from our subconscious to our conscious at the rate of ten thousand "frames" per second. If these are images of Christ-centered thoughts, they are a prayer. Since, in our waking moments, we are mostly involved in our outer world we are unaware of this activity. Nevertheless, we are affected by it.

*When I "see" images in my Two-way Prayer experience, how can I interpret their origin?*

In the illustration on page 143 four levels of the mind are represented in the columns. The first column represents the five senses. The impressions from our outer world are fed into the conscious mind, arousing our emotions. The experiences that arouse the greatest emotions are amplified and stored in the memory bank or subconscious computer. As we quiet the mind, sometimes these pictures or thoughts are played back to us like a tape recording. It may mean God wants us to examine the memory. We can ask him in prayer:
1) Why are you bringing this to my attention?
2) What am I to learn from that situation?
3) How could I have been more Christlike in handling it?
Next, ask yourself:
1) What are my *feelings* toward this replay of images or thoughts?"

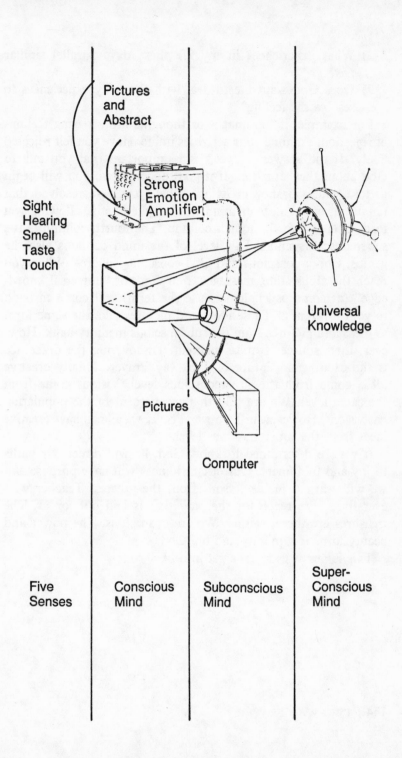

Pictures
and
Abstract

Sight
Hearing
Smell
Taste
Touch

Strong
Emotion
Amplifier

Universal
Knowledge

Pictures

Computer

Five
Senses

Conscious
Mind

Subconscious
Mind

Super-
Conscious
Mind

2) What experiences in my life these days parallel similar *feelings?*

3) Does God want me to deal with the daily experiences to resolve the feeling?

For example, if the images or thoughts are arousing feelings of rejection, examine your activities in life. Have you felt rejected lately? If the answer is "yes," it is important that you talk to God about that situation. If it goes uncorrected, you will begin to lose your vibrancy in living. When you have resolved that important emotion, your mind will be quieter still, allowing you to go deeper into the fourth column. The fourth column is the superconscious mind. This level of the mind contains also the genius, Christ-conscious and God-conscious spheres. When you reach the alpha state, messages from God, or "universal knowledge" (as some psychologists use the term) will come through to your awareness. These ideas and pictures take the same form as ideas and pictures from the subconscious memory bank. However, their source is quite different. Discovering the difference is the exciting adventure of Two-way Prayer. Totally creative ideas come from the superconscious level. Visions come from the same level. We are told that ten percent of the population has visions. However, in Two-way Prayer we all can have creative ideas from the superconscious level.

If we are determined to know God, he will direct our paths to joy and fulfillment. Our circumstances will have purpose and we will learn valuable lessons from the greatest Teacher who ever lived. We reach for the path that is laid out for us. The treasures are there waiting. We are champions. The power and beauty in us is a mighty and big God.

This is our world—let's get into it!

# *Notes*

## Introduction

[1] Diligent effort was made to learn of the author of this poem so proper credit could be given.

## Chapter 2

[1] Zaffuto, Anthony A. and Zaffuto, Mary Q., *Alphagenics: How to Use Your Brain Waves to Improve Your Life* (Garden City: Doubleday & Co., 1974), pp. 4 and 5.

[2] Benson, Herbert, *The Relaxation Response* (New York: William Morrow and Co., 1975), p. 82.

[3] Hill, Napoleon, and Stone, W. Clement, *Success Through a Positive Mental Attitude* (Englewood Cliffs, N.J.: Prentice-Hall, Inc., 1960), pp. 58, 59.

## Chapter 3

[1] Landorf, Joyce, *Joyce, I Feel Like I Know You* (Wheaton: Victor Books, 1976), p. 32.

## Chapter 4

[1] Peale, Norman Vincent, *A Guide to Confident Living* (Englewood Cliffs, N.J.: Prentice-Hall Inc., 1948), p. 79. Fawcett Crest Book.

## Chapter 5

[1] Lecture by Dr. Clifton King, Personal Development Center, Upland, CA, Oct. 1974.

## Chapter 6

[1] Names and places have been disguised to protect the principals in the story.

## Chapter 9

[1] Cramer, Raymond L., *The Psychology of Jesus and Mental Health* (Grand Rapids: Zondervan (Cowman), 1959), p. 188.

*Chapter 10*

[1] Peale, Norman Vincent, *A Guide to Confident Living*, p. 42.
[2] Harris, Thomas, M.D., *I'm O.K., You're O.K.* (Old Tappan, N.J.: Spire Books, 1967), pp. 25, 32.
[3] Zaffuto, Anthony and Mary, *Alphagenics*, p. 92.
[4] Brown, Barbara B., in Biofeedback Seminar at the University of Southern California, Irvine, California, Sept. 1974.
[5] Peale, Norman Vincent, *A Guide to Confident Living*, p. 37.

*Chapter 11*

[1] Benson, Herbert, *The Relaxation Response*, p. 64.
[2] Ibid., p. 67.

# Bibliography

Averill, J. R. "Automatic Response During Sadness and Mirth."
*Psychophysiology,* 1969.
Basmajian, J. V. and T. G. Simard. "Control and Training of Individual
Motor Units." *Science,* 1963, 741: pp. 440–441.
Benson, Herbert, M.D. *"The Relaxation Response."* New York: Morrow
& Co., Inc., 1975.
   An explanation in layman's terms of the physical changes and
   health benefits brought about by systematic relaxation techniques.
Benson, Herbert, H.D., and J. A. Herd. "Behavioral Induction of Arte-
rial Hypertension and Its Reversal." *American Journal of Physiol-
ogy,* 1969.
Brown, Barbara B., Ph.D. *New Mind, New Body, Biofeedback: New
Directions for the Mind.* New York: Harper & Row, 1974.
   Comprehensive results of the extensive research in biofeedback
   pioneered by Dr. Brown and her staff at the Veterans Administra-
   tion Hospital, Sepulveda, Calif. and the University of California
   in L.A. Medical Center. One of the best primary sources in research
   in biofeedback.
Cheraskin, E., M.D., and W.M. Ringsdorf, Jr., M.D., with Arline
Brecher. *Psycho-dietetics, Food as the Key to Emotional Health.*
New York: Stein and Day, 1974.
   Draws together research and findings on the correlation between
   diet and emotional health.
Cramer, Raymond L. *The Psychology of Jesus and Mental Health.* Grand
Rapids, Michigan: Zondervan (Cowman), 1958.
   Thorough psychological application of the Beatitudes and the im-
   pact they had on the lives of those who attempted to become
   integrated personalities by "living" the biblical principles.

Engel, B. T., S. P. Hansen. "Operant Condition of Heart Rate Slowings." *Psychophysiology,* 1966, 3: pp. 177–178.

Frankl, Viktor. *The Unconscious God: Psychotherapy and Theology.* New York: Simon and Schuster, 1976.

From a psychologist's point of view, Frankl presents convincing arguments that every person has in his unconscious mind a residual link with God.

Frankl, Viktor, *Man's Search for Meaning: An Introduction to Logotherapy.* Boston: Beaton Press, 1959.

Frankl's starkly honest experiences surviving in the World War II concentration camps serve as a basis for this book on logotherapy. It demonstrates the "will to meaning is fact not faith." Frankl, Europe's leading psychiatrist, possesses the unusual professional ability to write in layman's terms.

Green, E., A., and G. Murphy. "Feedback Techniques for Deep Relaxation," *Psychophysiology,* 1969, 6: pp. 371–377.

Guardine, Romano. *Prayer in Practice.* Garden City, New York: Doubleday & Co., Inc., 1963.

In this translation from the German, Guardine discusses the character of contemplative prayer and the preparation for prayer.

Hawkins, David, M.D., Linus Pauling, Ph.D. *Orthomolecular Psychology Treatment for Schizophrenia.* San Francisco: W. H. Freeman, 1973.

A detailed scientific documentation of case studies and research of nutritional effects on behavior.

Hill and Stone. *Success through a Positive Mental Attitude.* Englewood Cliffs, New Jersey: Prentice-Hall, Inc., 1972.

A motivational book for business containing case histories of men who put into practice the principles for success.

Jacobsen, E. *How to Relax and Have Your Baby.* New York: McGraw-Hill Book Co., 1965.

Step-by-step suggestions on how to relax in preparation for labor and delivery of a baby.

Jacobsen, E. *Progressive Relaxation.* Chicago: University of Chicago Press, 1958.

A major scientific work in the physiology of relaxation that led the way to effective techniques for natural childbirth and for dealing with tension-related diseases such as high blood pressure.

Jung, C. G. *Man and His Symbols.* Garden City, New York: Doubleday & Co., 1968.

An extensive work presenting the theory of inner images and their effect on man.

Jung, C. G. *Modern Man in Search of a Soul.* New York: Harcourt, Brace & World, Inc., 1933.

The levels of the mind and their importance in the growth and
development of the psyche.

Kelsey, Morton T. *The Other Side of Silence: A Guide to Christian
Meditation.* New York: Paulist Press, 1976.

A deeply theological and philosophical explanation of the inner
experience of prayer drawing in the findings of outstanding psychological authorities of the world from Sigmund Freud to Carl Rogers
to Rollo May.

Kelsey, Morton T. *Dreams, the Dark Speech of the Spirit, A Christian
Interpretation.* Garden City, New York: Doubleday & Co., Inc.,
1968.

A Christian interpretation of dreams as "windows" to the unconscious and spiritual world and essence of God himself. Traces
dreams from Old Testament through New Testament to today's
Christian attitudes. A fascinating study by a minister of a church
that maintains its own psychological clinic.

Laubach, Frank C. *Open Windows, Swinging Doors.* Glendale, California: Regal, 1975.

The spiritual diary of a missionary in the Philippines who traces
his experiments with the idea of being conscious of God every
second of the day. Drawing closer to God as a result, Dr. Laubach
describes two-way prayer.

Leebman, Joshus Loth. *Peace of Mind.* New York: The New American
Library, Inc., 1973.

Presents crucial questions dealing with conscience, love, fear, grief,
and God. A rabbi discusses the complementary factors of religion
and psychology.

Mattola, Anthony. *The Spiritual Exercises of St. Ignatius.* Garden City,
New York: Doubleday & Co., 1964.

From the translated notebooks of this sixteenth century man of
God comes a practical guide to contemplative prayer experiences.

Nowlis, D. P. and J. Kameya. "The Control of Electroencephalographic
Alpha Rhythm Through Auditory Feedback and Associate Mental
Activity." *Psychophysiology,* 1970, 6: pp. 480–484.

Osborne, Cecil. *The Art of Understanding Yourself.* Grand Rapids,
Michigan: Zondervan, 1967.

Blends religion and psychology in simple language that challenges
man's search for identity to be found inwardly.

Peale, Norman V. *A Guide to Confident Living.* Greenwich, Connecticut:
Fawcett Crest, 1948.

Introduces the results of "creative silence" and analyzes our hin-
drances to creativity.

Peers, E. Alison. *Interior Castle: St. Teresa of Avella.* Garden City,
New York: Doubleday & Co., Inc., 1961.

Written to her Sisters, an early (1577) account of St. Teresa's devotional on prayer and her struggles for union with God. Limited to the sixteenth century knowledge of God and the mind.

Reed, W. S. *Surgery of the Soul.* Old Tappan, New Jersey: Revell, 1975. Cases from a physician and surgeon which illustrate that faith, or its lack, has a physical impact on the whole man, in illness and in health.

Richardson, A. *Mental Imagery.* New York: Springer Publishing Company, 1969.
Mechanism and examples of internal images describing the steps of relaxation to improve visualization and remove extraneous stimuli.

Samuels, M., and N. Samuels. *Seeing with the Mind's Eye the History, Techniques and Uses of Visualization.* (Co-published by) New York: Random House Inc.,: and Berkeley, California: The Bookworks, 1975.
The direct path between the mind and the body, the inner and outer world, our human self and divine source, our conscious and subconscious.

Sanford, John A. *The Kingdom Within.* Philadelphia and New York: J. B. Lippincott Co., 1970.
Refocuses the words of Jesus on the inner life for a rediscovery of the personal and creative side of Christianity.

Schuller, Robert. *Move Ahead with Possibility Thinking.* Garden City, New York: Prentice-Hall, 1962.
With examples applied to business, the book emphasizes the healthy mind and its control as the secret to success and creativity.

Schuller, Robert. *Self Love.* New York: Hawthorn Books, Inc., 1969.
Differentiates self-respect from selfishness and tells how to build a wholesome self-esteem in others as well as in one's self.

Schuller, Robert. *You Can Become the Person You Want to Be.* New York: Hawthorn Books, Inc., 1973.
Explains self-defeating thought patterns and gives examples of people who have overcome their destructive inner mechanisms to find power and beauty in their lives. Written on an easy-to-understand level.

Schuller, Robert. *Your Future Is Your Friend.* New Canaan, Connecticut: Keats Publishing, Inc., 1974.
A line by line living message on Psalm 23 containing God's promise for guidance and victory.

Strong, James, S.T.D., L.L.D. *The Exhaustive Concordance of the Bible.* New York: Abingdon-Cokesbury Press.
The definitive scholarly source of denotative and connotative translations of the words used in scripture.

Zaffuto, Anthony A., with Mary A. Zaffuto. *Alphagenics: How to Use Your Brain Waves to Improve Your Life.* Garden City, New York: Doubleday & Co., Inc., 1974.
The results of the research done in the alpha brain wave. Includes alphagenics training in layman's terms.